A History of
World Communism

A History of World Communism

F W Deakin, H Shukman and H T Willetts

BARNES & NOBLE

BOOKS

10 East 53d St., New York 10022

(a division of Harper & Row Publishers, Inc.)

© F. W. Deakin, H. Shukman and H. T. Willetts

Published in Great Britain by
Weidenfeld and Nicolson
11 St John's Hill, London, SW11.

Published in the U.S.A. 1975 by
Harper & Row Publishers, Inc.
Barnes & Noble Import Division.

ISBN 0-06-491623-5

Library of Congress Number 75-2866

Printed in Great Britain by
Willmer Brothers Limited, Birkenhead.

Contents

Illustrations

part 1
The Three Internationals

1

The Forerunners

Communism is a social ideal of great antiquity. Aristotle mentions a still earlier thinker who recommended common ownership as cure for poverty, and Plato thought it a fitting way of life for the intellectual aristocrats who would rule his republic. The Pythagoreans, the Essenes of Judaea, the earliest Christians and a host of heretics from the Manichaeans to the Anabaptists thought private property incompatible with brotherly love and spiritual purity. Monastic asceticism often demanded the renunciation of personal property. In post-Renaissance Europe Thomas More's *Utopia* and Campanella's *Civitas Solis* pictured imaginary societies whose prosperity and happiness rested on communist principles. Amongst the French luminaries of the eighteenth century Mably condemned private property as the source of class divisions and an obstacle to good citizenship. Communist ideas were alien to most of the ideologists of the French Revolution, but there were some amongst the Jacobins who saw a contradiction between equality of rights and inequalities of wealth. Boissel, for instance, thought that distribution according to needs (a concept taken by the eighteenth century Utopian writer Morelli from the Acts of the Apostles) was a condition of social equality; Marat attacked the aristocracy of money and held that equal rights implied equal enjoyments. The communist trend in Jacobinism reached its climax in the 'Conspiracy of Equals' led by Gracchus Babeuf (guillotined in 1796), who wanted to eliminate all differences except those of age and sex.

In the first decades of the nineteenth century the social ravages of the industrial revolution, and the complacent unconcern of governments and of the surgent middle class for its victims, provoked an intellectual rebellion. These years saw a bewildering profusion of political and economic works now conventionally grouped together as 'socialist' or 'communist': though there is no

3

infallible rule for applying one adjective rather than the other to each particular work, and both were refused by some of the writers in question. This corpus of political literature is united by rejection of the harsh norms of laissez-faire capitalism, on which bourgeois political economists seemed to confer the status of natural laws: and by its quest for means to ensure the material well-being and the human dignity of the 'most numerous and the poorest class'.

The phrase belonged to Henri de St Simon (1760–1825). As systematized by Bazard, the most influential of his followers, St Simonism called for the abolition of hereditary wealth – 'the privilege of levying a toll on the labour of others' – and the pooling of all 'instruments of labour, land and capital in a social fund'. The St Simonians were not egalitarians. Devotees of progress, boundlessly optimistic about the benefits to be expected from science and industry, they condemned above all the wastefulness of the existing economic order, its failure to put capital into the ablest hands, its lack of 'grand designs' to harmonize the labours of society. Resources must be exploited 'hierarchically', the state assigning tasks to its citizens according to their capacity, and rewarding them according to their work. The St Simonians showed no fear that the all-possessing state would become a monstrous tyranny: indeed, it would, they held, cease to be a state in the ordinary sense and become a mere 'association of toilers', a term in which they included their highly rewarded scientists and organizers of production. This transformation would be eased by the disappearance of war – in the 1830s the St Simonians could still convince themselves that Napoleon's wars had been the last of the great European upheavals. Humanity was 'gravitating' towards universal association, and the exploitation of man by man would give way to common, and concerted, 'exploitation of the globe'.

The St Simonians relied on propaganda, especially amongst intellectuals, and the pressure of public opinion on governments, for the success of their cause. Louis Blanc (1813–82), also a devotee of state socialism, believed in more direct political action. Those who would liberate the proletariat must win control of the state machine, either through success in elections, or by more impatient means. The state would then take on itself the role of 'banker of the poor', organizing 'national workshops'. The enthusiasm of the workers, and the economies they would make, would drive private enterprises out of business, and unite all industry (and agriculture) in a network of self-governing producers' associations. The state would shortly become a mere regulator, not interfering in the internal activities of the associations: 'the machine once set up would work by itself'. Initially, the producers would be paid according to their work, but later men would come to regard superior talents as a measure of their obligations to society, not of their claims on it, and distribution would be according to need.

France in the 1830s and early 1840s was the main breeding-ground of communist as well as socialist ideas. The proliferating communist sects, which (according to one of their enemies, Proudhon) may have won as many as 100,000 adherents, were distinguished by their overriding concern with egalitarian distribution. Some of them, including the most influential of all, Cabet, were sustained by a belief that enlightenment inevitably made men more altruistic, some relied on the authority of religion and found their warranty in the gospels, some held that a rational reconstruction of the economy could once and for all curb the freeplay of human egoism. As a rule, they expected, like St Simon and Blanc, to achieve their aims by propaganda. But on the left wing of materialist communism Pillot was for establishing communism by force and treating its opponents like madmen, and even the 'neo-Catholic' communist, the Abbé Constant, at times favoured the removal of obstacles to Christian love by violence.

The early nineteenth century offered opportunities for practical experiments in creating models for the good society. Pioneering communist colonies were planted, by Cabet amongst others, in the American wilderness, and rapidly collapsed. But it seemed possible, in a period when trade and industry were expanding fast, to establish oases of the good life in Europe too. The prolific fantasist Charles Fourier preached withdrawal from the unjust society into 'phalansteries', which would afford their inhabitants such freedom and material wellbeing that they would eventually draw the whole world into a federation of self-governing communities, presided over by the 'Omniaque' of Constantinople. Few could accept fully the insanely elaborate system of this sciolist mystic. But he gave a powerful stimulus to two important lines of speculation: on the possibility of building a just society by voluntary association and on the means of ensuring the fullest gratification of psychological as well as material needs. 'Fourierism', in variants which the prophet would not have recognized, spread throughout Europe and to the United States, and was the first 'socialist' school to influence significantly the Russian intelligentsia.

The idea of action to create a just society without resort to or concern for the state reached its apogee in P. J. Proudhon, the founder of modern anarchism. Priding himself on his plebeian origin, he claimed, with much justice, to understand the common people and their needs better than any bourgeois intellectual. The passion for individual freedom, and intolerance of all authority ('– always deny!') inspired in him not only hatred of the state but contempt for tyrannous socialism à la Louis Blanc and for levelling communism. A fanatical atheist and materialist ('God is evil!') he is none the less scarcely more practical, and is much less consistent, than the mystical Fourier. 'Property is theft' is his best remembered utterance. Yet he saw in property the essential safeguard of human freedom and dignity, the only protection against political impression. What he meant to condemn was the use of property to levy rent on the labour of others, and he busily evolved schemes for the replacement of money by direct exchange of products and for the creation of credit by the workers themselves, banded together for mutual support. In the mutualist society there would be no room and no need for centralized economic organization, still less for the state. Communes would be self-governing, and large industrial enterprises would be to the worker 'what the hive is to bees, their tool, their home, their country, their territory, their property'. Laws would disappear, replaced by freely concluded contracts. The nation state would give way to a free federation of sovereign communes. War would become obsolete, because whereas the centralized state is inevitably expansionist the commune lacks the means of aggression. Proudhonism is muddled, contradictory, chimerical. But his attitudes and ideals, his detestation of 'governmentalism', his disbelief in 'political' methods of reform, whether through the authoritarian state or formal democracy, his rejection of law as a tyrannical imposition, his exaltation of individual freedom and small self-governing associations, lived on in the anarchist movement which provided the fiercest critics and at times the most powerful challenge to state socialism in its mature, Marxist form.

A fourth important strand in what is loosely called the socialist tradition was woven by Auguste Blanqui (1805–81), who earned the soubriquet 'L'Eferme' by spending thirty-seven years of his life in gaol. He began his political career in Carbonarist secret societies, vowed to the establishment of a liberal republic by insurrection. But by 1834 Blanqui was proclaiming that the republic would merely supply the political machinery which the workers would use for their own social liberation. Conspiratorial activity became for him merely a means for preparing the creation of mass revolutionary organizations when circumstances allowed. Disgust with the liberal government thrown up by the revolution of 1848 cured him of any lingering belief in bourgeois democracy. Only socialism was capable of transforming modern society, and only by means of a revolution to overthrow the privileged classes. The revolutionary government must disarm the bourgeoisie, disband its armies and its bureaucracy, renounce universal suffrage. A proletarian dictatorship would 'maintain continuous revolution' until the realization of communism, which must be the final form of organization of the human race.

Communist and revolutionary ideas found an eager audience amongst the German artisans and craftsmen in Belgium, Switzerland and France. Secret societies flourished amongst them, and to one of these, the League of the Just, dominated by Wilhelm Weitling, Marx's Communist League can trace its descent. Weitling's ideal society was a federation of communities of craftsmen, with a Supreme Council of Three comprising the greatest geniuses of 'philosophical medicine', physics and engineering, at its head. Many of his reforms look like a mere change of labels: government would be replaced by administration, laws by obligations, elections by examinations, money by labour coupons. But in the early 1840s his attacks on formal democracy, and his call for the organization of the working class in revolutionary struggle, had a certain influence on Marx. Simultaneously, Weitling introduced Bakunin to notions which were to have a great future in the anarchist tradition: the deliberate promotion of chaos, the disorganization of society, to prepare the ground for revolution, and the use of the lumpenproletariat – rootless, déclassé elements in society, including vagabonds and criminals – as a revolutionary striking force.

Marx's career as a revolutionary organizer began in competition with Weitling. Through the 'Communist Corresponding Committees' established in 1846 Marx and his friends wrested sufficient support from the League of the Just to set up, in June 1847, the

Communist League. Its aims were defined as the overthrow of the bourgeoisie, the rule of the proletariat, the abolition of a society based on class antagonism and the formation of a society without classes or private property. The slogan 'Proletariat of All Lands Unite!' made its appearance on the first number of the League's journal. The second congress of the League, at the end of the year, commissioned Marx to expound its aims more fully. The result was *The Communist Manifesto*, published in February 1848. It was too late, and too outré, to influence the revolutionary events of that year, but before long it gained acceptance as the foundation document of scientific socialism.

2

Marx and Scientific Socialism

Communists today, for all their diversities, all claim descent from Marx. His work was described by Lenin as a synthesis of all that was best in German philosophy, French socialist thought and English political economy. One effect of his feat of synthesis was to complicate still further the task of distinguishing between 'communism' and 'socialism': for the only clearly communistic component of the Marxist system is its ultimate ideal, while the means proposed for its achievement are an unstable mixture of elements from the state socialist and the insurrectionist traditions. 'Scientific socialism', provided the inverted commas are retained, expresses the essence of Marx's ideas more satisfactorily than 'communism'.

Marx showed an affectionate tolerance towards many of those socialist and communist pioneers with whom he had no personal contact, but he dismissed their approach as Utopian and idealistic, in contrast to his own scientific and materialistic views. Indeed, if we search the works of his predecessors for some assurance that a society of brothers and equals is feasible we shall find nothing weightier than a belief in the essential goodness of man, or in the progressive triumph of reason. Marx on the contrary held that socialism would replace capitalism not because all reasonable men of goodwill would so wish, but because of economic determinism: the evolution of capitalism itself made the change inevitable.

Marx's vision of an ineluctable historical process transcending human will and consciousness was part of his German philosophical heritage. But, unlike his first philosophical idol, Hegel, he found the moving force of history not in an endlessly evolving world soul but in the interaction between man and his environment. The way in which a society provides for its material needs (the means of production) determines the ownership of property and the class structure, which in turn determines the system of government. Further, the economic and institutional structure determine man's philosophical, religious, ethical and artistic values ('being determines consciousness'). Expressed in anti-Cartesian terms this 'I am, therefore I think' concept reflects Marx's environmental approach to the way man forms his values and beliefs.

Institutions and ideas ultimately adjust themselves to changes in the means of production, but not automatically and smoothly. At some point the further growth of society's wealth demands changes in the existing pattern of property relationships and the institutions established for their protection. No ruling class surrenders its position without a fight, and the class most vitally interested in the reconstruction of society must therefore embark on revolutionary struggle. The outcome can only be the surrender or destruction of the old regime, since its rivals can mobilize the grievances of all classes against it, and since the cause of the rising class is for the time being that of society at large.

Marx distinguished four historical–social formations, corresponding to successive levels of economic development: the primitive communist, the servile, the feudal and the bourgeois. A fifth and final phase lay ahead: as feudalism had superseded slavery, as bourgeois capitalism was progressively liquidating feudalism, just as surely would socialism grow out of and forcibly replace capitalism.

Marx had boldy stood Hegel on his head to make of his teaching a materialist philosophy of history. He adapted Hegel's form – the dialectical process of conflict by which each historical stage develops into the next, then deleted the idealist content and added his materialism. He had just as confidently synthesized those elements of earlier socialist theories which seemed to him realistic, and discarded the rest as Utopian fantasy. But his supreme act of intellectual daring was to turn against the bourgeoisie the most formidable of its idealogical weapons – the science of political economy. Marx argued that capitalism contained within itself the seeds of its own destruction. Using the Hegelian dialectic this is the *antithesis*, which evolves from the *thesis* (capitalism); from there the two merge (*synthesis*), thereby forming the next and higher stage of history – socialism. The fierce competition for profits would concentrate ownership of the means of production in ever fewer hands, swell the ranks of the dispossessed and exploited, intensify the exploitation of the working masses. Technological advance, stimulated by competition, would aggravate exploitation, since the capitalist made profits only by withholding from the worker part of the additional value which labour alone created. This theory, a borrowing from Ricardo, is called 'the labour theory of value'. To pay for the increasingly expensive plant which the competitive struggle made necessary the capitalist must withhold more and more. Capitalism therefore doomed the masses to progressive impoverishment. This is a major aspect of the inner contradiction as antithesis, of capitalism. At the same time, by concentrating industry and accustoming the worker to social modes of production, capitalism prepared the ground for socialism. The new society beginning to take shape within the old would eventually burst out of its antiquated and cramping shell. In political terms, this meant that the exacerbated worker would rebel against his enfeebled and decadent exploiters, replace private ownership by public ownership of the means of production, and the bourgeois state by a dictatorship of the proletariat.

This highest of social formations would pass through two phases. The *function* of the proletarian dictatorship was limited: it would complete the expropriation of the expropriators, it would expand production (which capitalism in its death throes had inhibited) to the point at which the toilers' needs could be fully satisfied and it, the state, would cease to exist. Beyond socialism, characterized by proletarian dictatorship and distribution of (as yet inadequate) resources according to work performed, lay the classless communist society, in which the state – never more than an instrument for the dictatorial rule of a particular class over other classes – would 'wither away', and goods, now abundant, would be distributed according to needs. This transition from socialism to communism would be peaceful, as there are no minor contradictions, or antithesis in the former for unlike all previous states it would be a dictatorship of the majority. All previous history, which was merely a record of class struggles, would seem to be prehistory, a mere prelude to the maturity of society, when man would no longer struggle against man but when all mankind, united at last in a free, fraternal association, would concentrate its whole effort on the struggle for ever greater mastery over the material world.

Some of Marx's ideas, from the concept that economic relationships are the basis of all relationships to several of his specific recommendations in *The Communist Manifesto*, have sunk so deeply into the modern consciousness that it is easy to underrate the brilliance and originality of his achievement and to concentrate on those elements in his thought which have not stood the test of time. Marx himself attempted no synthesis, and it is to Engels and others that we must look for a synoptic view of Marxism. None the less, though his work bristles with loose ends, its leading ideas form an integral system. As such it is very much a product of his time. The very idea of a total, monistic explanation of human history, the attempt to find the explanation in laws of social development comparable in their immutability and universality to the laws governing the evolution of the physical world, the unbounded optimism about the capacity of the human intellect and the future of human society, place Marx firmly in the mid-nineteenth century, For socialists and communists of all schools – if they would listen – Marx had an answer to all doubts and a solution for all difficulties. Those who were troubled by the failure of the French Revolution to usher in freedom, equality and fraternity could learn that the revolution had served its true purpose in replacing feudal absolutism by the rule of bourgeois capitalism, which would prepare the ground for proletarian revolution and socialism. Romantics who longed for a new uprising to complete the work of 1793, and were repeatedly disillusioned, could learn that the final revolution depended on the maturity of the economic conditions for it and the growth of a strong and politically conscious proletariat, processes which, according to Marx, were well advanced. Those who believed that the working class must struggle for its emancipation within the existing framework of society and using the existing institutions – bourgeois parliaments, trades unions, the free press – could find common ground with Marx, for he regarded this day to day struggle as a necessary part of political education and revolutionary training. But he was also in qualified agreement with those who placed all their hopes on the summary seizure of state power, for he too believed that only revolution could effect a radical reconstruction of society, with the proviso that it must be the work of the politically conscious masses, not of a conspiratorial elite. The widest rift on the European left was between politically minded socialists – revolutionary or non-revolutionary – and anarchists, who rejected the day-to-day political struggle and thought the idea of a socialist state a contradiction in terms. Even with the anarchists he had in common the ultimate ideal – that of a classless and stateless society – though Proudhon and Bakunin, whom Marx pursued with relentless ideological fury, saw a fatal incongruity between this end and the political means proposed for its attainment.

The realistic elements in Marx's view of history and his critique of contemporary society, the tactical flexibility which he legitimated in the present, and his unbounded optimism for the future ensured for him a wider and more durable influence than any of his predecessors. Though his system was eclectic its leading principles were firmly integrated. It was these leading principles, and his method of social analysis, for which Marx claimed scientific validity. He certainly did not pretend that every word he wrote was sacrosanct, or that he had an immediate and definitive answer to all problems of social analysis and political tactics. His impatience with scholasticism once drew from him the protest that he was 'not a Marxist'. He believed in the 'dialectical unity of theory and practice', which meant that political hypotheses, like those of science, must be tested and refined empirically. He offered no precise revolutionary timetable. He did not suppose that socialism would triumph everywhere by the same means or at precisely the same stage of economic development. His assertion that no social formation is superseded until its capacity for growth is exhausted was to be taken together with another dictum, that revolutions occur when the ruling class can no longer rule and its subjects will no longer be ruled in the old way. To Marx, there was no doubt that the skill and flexibility of the capitalist state, and the level of revolutionary consciousness of the workers, as well as the mounting economic difficulties of capitalism, would decide the moment of revolutionary transition. Writing as a political economist, he offered a model of the way in which capitalism would develop to the point of senile collapse. As a political thinker he had no doubt that the exacerbated proletariat would act to accelerate the collapse of bourgeois society. He was always clear that the specific forms of socialist revolution would vary from country to country. In Britain, he once suggested, socialism might be established more or less peacefully, because the central state machine (by which Marx always meant primarily its organs of coercion) was so sketchy. On another occasion, he envisaged, in apparent contradiction with basic principles, a successful revolution to establish socialism in Russia – an agrarian country where the industrial proletariat was as yet utterly insignificant, but where the autocratic state had no solid social base – provided that it was quickly followed by proletarian revolutions in more advanced countries. Germany again was a special case, and Marx came to see it as the liveliest hope of revolutionary socialism, because a weak and politically timid bourgeoisie was caught between an authoritarian ruling class and an impatient proletariat.

Marx's breadth and empiricism made his system a flexible tool of historical interpretation, but an ambiguous guide to action. Indeed, some, like the Russian P. M. Tkachev – whose belief that revolutions are made not by masses but by small groups of expertly trained and determined men makes him a tactical predecessor of Lenin – saw it as a recipe for inaction. To some of Marx's critics it seemed that triumphant bourgeois democracy might prove a barrier against revolution rather than an approach road to it, that participation in bourgeois politics might sap the revolutionary vigour of socialists and domesticate them. Yet Marxism left much room for special interpretations and diversity of action: insurrectionists, syndicalists and parliamentary socialists could all find in Marx some warrant for their views. In Marx's lifetime his theories were never the platform of any substantial political party. After his death a number of parties called themselves Marxist, but pious lip-service to Marx was commoner than revolutionary fervour. The spirit of revolutionary Marxism burnt most fiercely in backward European countries where isolated socialist groups were denied a parliamentary arena or a mass following. It is from the October Revolution in Russia that we must date the emergence of revolutionary Marxism as a political force of worldwide significance.

3

The First International

Communism was by its very nature uncompromisingly internationalist. How could its ideals be realized, how in particular could the state 'be relegated to the museum of antiquities beside the spinning wheel and the bronze axe' in a world scored by fortified frontiers? This was one of many obvious points on which Marx and Engels were not precise enough for Stalin: in 1939, although no one had asked him openly why the Soviet Union needed a uniquely powerful state machine, Stalin declared that Engels's statements on the withering away of the state tacitly assumed the establishment of socialism in a number of countries. But Marx and Engels had not needed to qualify their teaching on the future of the state in this way because to begin with they had never expected the triumph of revolutionary socialism in a single country. In the *Communist Manifesto* they declared that 'united action of the leading civilized countries at least is one of the first conditions for the emancipation of the proletariat': and Engels later identified Germany, France and Britain as the decisive countries.

The national interests which divided the world were, in Marx's view, merely those of ruling groups, which in the advanced countries meant those of the bourgeoisie. Indeed, the modern state was the creation and instrument of capitalism. The working man, said Marx, had no country. Unlike the capitalists, the common people had no interest in the perpetuation of international strife, in the exploitation of nation by nation. And so, unlike the bourgeoisie of the world, the proletariat could pool its strength for common ends. The *Communist Manifesto* ends with a ringing summons. 'Workers of the world unite – you have nothing to lose but your chains!' Marx and Engels believed that capitalism had in fact already begun the process of world unification by enlacing all countries in a single system of commerce and communications. Unity in this sense meant involvement in a single complex of conflicts. It could be converted into harmony and universal co-operation only by proletarian revolution. A further assurance that the proletariat of different countries would be drawn into concerted revolutionary action was found in the escalating series of economic crises which Marx dated from 1825: they could not be contained within national borders, their ravages bore more and more heavily on ever widening circles of the proletariat, the peasantry and the petty bourgeoisie in many countries. The internationalization of economic crisis would naturally internationalize rebellion against capitalism.

The arguments merely refined and modernized a faith implanted in revolutionaries by the greatest political rebellion in modern history. It was taken for granted that just as the repercussions of the great French Revolution had been felt throughout Europe and beyond, so would some future rebellion start a train of simultaneous explosions in several countries. If this passionate hope, which Marx and Engels shared with revolutionaries of other persuasions, seems unrealistic in retrospect we should remember that it was reflected in the nightmares of Europe's rulers. The 'spectre of communism' which Marx saw 'stalking Europe' looms large in the police archives of his time. The post-Napoleonic period had been punctuated by simultaneous revolutionary flurries in several countries at a time. But it was the turbulent year of 1848 that seemed most nearly to confirm the internationalist thesis: the first revolutionary tremor was felt in Italy, the epicentre of the quake proved to be Paris, major upheavals followed in Germany and Austria, and the shockwaves radiated even to Britain. These of course were bourgeois revolutions. Their simultaneity was not explained by any spirit of international solidarity amongst the bourgeoisie, but by emulation, by the temptation to exploit the momentary distraction of reactionary governments, and also by the disturbing effects of the latest crisis of over-production and by crop failures in a number of countries. Genuine internationalism was confined to the communists and the advanced sections of the working class. Marx at least never lost hope of another European revolution in which the proletariat would play a greater role, but there was to be no repetition of 1848, and no sequence of events which even the most sanguine Marxist could see as a revolution of international scope before the Bolshevik seizure of power in 1917.

The failures and hollow victories of 1848 prompted Marx and

Engels to enlarge on certain of their ideas which were to have great importance in the future. They had previously recognized that the revolutionary bourgeoisie must rely partly on other discontented classes, that the resultant coalition is unstable, since bourgeois interests and those of the masses will at some point conflict, and that in such a situation the bourgeoisie will turn against its allies, either concluding a compromise with the old ruling class (as in seventeenth-century England), or setting up an elitist bourgeois dictatorship (as in France after 1795). In 1848 the bourgeoisie, frightened by the radicalism of its allies, collapsed in Italy, sought salvation first in military repression and then in bourgeois monarchy in France, and reached a *modus vivendi* with the remnants of feudalism in Germany. The proletariat in short could not trust the bourgeoisie even to carry through its own revolution to the establishment of a democratic republic: liberals would always betray their professed political ideals if their realization carried with it a threat to bourgeois economic interests. But 1848 had shown that the political awareness of the masses was growing, their demands becoming more vociferous, even in countries where completion of the bourgeois revolution seemed a distant prospect. From these observations Marx concluded that proletarian revolutionary forces might grow within a bourgeois revolutionary situation to the point at which they would change its character and determine its outcome. This theory of 'permanent revolution', first expounded in Marx's Appeal to the Communist League in 1850, is difficult to reconcile with the more usual Marxist prognosis, that the proletarian movement would mature within the milieu created by successful bourgeois revolution.

The notion of 'permanent revolution' would naturally recommend itself to the more impatient of Marx's followers, and in the early twentieth century two of them – Lenin and Trotsky – would put forward their own variants of it. It would be rash to dismiss them as less 'orthodox' than the gradualist Mensheviks, with their meticulous concern for the traditional Marxian 'prerequisites' of proletarian revolution. The opposition between the Bolshevik and Menshevik trends was a polarization of an unresolved contradiction in Marx himself.

In Italy and Germany in 1848 bourgeois revolution was inextricably bound up with the movement for national unification, while in the Hapsburg lands the main revolutionary impetus came from the struggle of Austria's Hungarian and Slav subjects for national independence. Marx and Engels gave much thought to the inter-action between nationalist and proletarian movements. The drive for national unification had their sympathy – and in the case of Germany their enthusiasm exposed them to unwarranted suspi-cions of chauvinism. Their calculation was that only national unification would permit the rapid economic development of those countries, and so the growth of a strong proletariat, and that in a fragmented nation the class struggle would be muffled and dis-torted by illusions of a common national interest. Similarly, they supported the struggle for independence of all subject peoples capable of independent nationhood. (Engels was for a time less sure than Marx that the Poles came into this category.) Here, their argument was that while a whole people was held in subjection the proletariat would make common cause with 'its own bour-geoisie'. Moreover, Marx and Engels thought that in the proleta-riat of an imperial nation the revolutionary urge was weakened by their complicity in oppression: as proof of this they would point to England, and the effects of its oppression of Ireland on the English working class. The tempo of proletarian revolution, then, would be affected by changes in the political map of Europe. Though Marx looked no further, Engels late in life gave some attention to the future of colonial peoples. But he remained obstinately European in his outlook, so sure of the civilizing mission of his native continent that he envisaged proletarian states exercising some sort of tutelage over the colonies of their bour-geois predecessors, and preparing them for emancipation.

The *Communist Manifesto*, published in 1848, had little influence on the events of that year, and according to Engels was noticed only by a few Germans. In the following decade Marx's economic and social theories attracted little interest except among revolu-tionary intellectuals. His more original works were not easy to read or assimilate. As late as 1867, his friend the revolutionary poet Freiligrath innocently praised the first volume of *Capital* as a useful handbook for young businessmen, and in 1872 the Russian censor authorized a translation of that work on the grounds that it was too academic to be politically dangerous. Between 1850 and 1864, a barren and disheartening period for revolutionaries, Marx divided his time between research and bread and butter journal-ism, specializing in the exposure of European diplomatic machinations for the scandalized edification of Americans. It was the First International, founded in London in September 1864, which made Marx a celebrity. His work as the most determined organizer and most eloquent agitator in its ranks forced the 'Red Doctor's' ideas on the attention of the nascent workers' movement throughout Europe.

Popular agitation in support of Poland's struggle for independence, and of the Northern cause in the American Civil War, generated much of the heat which welded the International together, and one of its main functions was to provide a platform from which members could assert a distinct working-class view on current international issues. Beyond this, each member organization saw the International as a means for enhancing its influence in its own country. The English trade unionists were intent on reinforcing an already strong position, and some of them lost interest in the International when an alliance with English liberalism seemed politically more rewarding. Some members, notably the French, sought comfort and support in their struggle for recognition at home. Some members, as for instance the Russian section admitted in 1868, and domiciled in Geneva, relied on the International for assurance of their existence.

The foundation manifesto and the statutes (finally approved in 1871) were drafted by Marx. He declared that the emancipation of the working class must be won by the working class itself, that the road to economic emancipation lay through political power, and that the condition of success was practical and theoretical collaboration between the most advanced countries. In setting out these basic principles Marx exercised unusual tact in order to attract the widest possible support. Even so, rivalries between sects limited the appeal of the International. Blanqui and his followers, for instance, held aloof from an organization in which Proudhonists at first played a prominent part. Marx did not attempt to analyse the divisions within socialism. He seems to have hoped that solidarity against the common enemy would hold incongruous groups together while a common ideology evolved. Thus, in the ringing peroration of the *Manifesto* he stressed the need for unity 'in the face of a foreign policy which pursuing criminal ends plays on national prejudices and in predatory wars sheds the blood and squanders the wealth of the people'. The working class must 'master the secrets of international policy, keep watch on the diplomatic activity of its governments, and where necessary counteract it with all means at its disposal'. The struggle for a just and moral foreign policy 'constitutes part of the general struggle for liberation of the working class'.

The statutes provided for annual congresses of the International, but also for a permanent co-ordinating body called the General Council. Its membership was rather vaguely defined as 'workers from the various countries represented in the International Association', and though elected by congress it could co-opt additional members. It was through this body that Marx came to dominate the International. Nominally, he was merely the corresponding secretary for the German section, and later also for the wraithlike Russian section. He owed his commanding position to his generally recognized intellectual superiority, his skill in drafting cogent resolutions and ringing declarations, and also to his energy in political infighting within the International. The Association relied heavily on the willingness of Marx and other émigrés to give a great deal of time for little reward, its revenues being in Marx's words 'a constantly increasing negative quantity'. Their compensation was that as displaced persons with no strong local base they could achieve eminence and gratify their passion for organizational work only in an international body. Apart from his émigré friends (some of whom turned against him when his policies became a threat to their own standing) Marx could, to begin with, generally depend on British and German support. Moreover, he, Engels and other congenial notabilities were often entrusted with the mandates of outlying sections. As a result Marx was able for some years to weather the ideological storms which blew up at congresses and to keep congress decisions as a rule close to the Marxist line. He was rather less successful in his impatient efforts to make the International a homogeneous and disciplined body.

According to the Statutes the function of the General Council was to ensure that 'the workers of the country are constantly kept informed of the movement of their class in other countries'; that 'the examination of social conditions in various countries of Europe should be carried on simultaneously and under a single direction'; 'that questions raised in one society but presenting a general interest should be discussed by all'; and that 'when immediate practical steps are required, as for instance in the case of international conflicts, member societies of the Association should act simultaneously and in the same way'. A much less self-assured and impatient man than Marx would not have found it easy to draw the line between co-ordination and direction. The statutes provided that 'in all appropriate cases the General Council must take on itself the initiative in introducing proposals to the various national or local societies', which clearly meant that at any moment a member organization might find itself forced to accept or reject the majority opinion of the London representatives of all member organizations. Moreover, the organizational role of the General Council steadily grew. In 1869 for instance it added to its powers of recruitment the right to expel member organizations.

In the early years of rapid recruitment the International allowed its members considerable ideological latitude, and admitted rival and incompatible groups from the same country. But as the organizational ambitions of the General Council grew, it became more discriminating and pressed harder for conformity. It was from the start intended that as far as local conditions permitted the groups in any particular country should try to unite in a national organization, and in 1871 Marx succeeded in adding to the statutes the requirement that the proletariat must unite in 'its own political party'. The drive for unification met with very little success, but it multiplied the opportunities for intervention by the General Council in local squabbles and increased friction within the International. Marx of course generally favoured the groups ideologically closest to himself, and his manoeuvres provoked growing dissatisfaction with his 'dictatorial' behaviour. The location of the General Council in London had helped Marx to establish his hold on it. Harassed by the unruly French representatives in London, he thought of transferring the Council's seat to Geneva. But Switzerland shortly became a stronghold of Bakuninism, which with its insistence on loose federative organizations and on social revolution without patient political preparation, was anathema to Marx. By 1872, he had despaired of converting the International into an effective and disciplined body, and grudged every minute devoted to sterile political squabbling at the expense of his scholarly work. He contrived the transfer of the General Council to New York, where it was too remote to be effectual, but also beyond the reach of his rivals. For the remaining years of its existence the International was a shadow of itself.

In retrospect the unresolved problems of the First International and the disagreements within its ranks have a symptomatic importance for the whole future of international communism. The dictatorial behaviour of the General Council was not merely an expression of Marx's imperious and impatient temperament. It was inherent in any attempt to unite effectively a large number of groups with distinctive ideological and national personalities, operating in very different social and political circumstances. Unanimity was attainable in a moment of revolutionary excitement, as the response of the International to the Paris Commune showed in 1871. Concerted practical action was sometimes possible, as for instance in measures to prevent the import of labour from one country to break a strike in another. But the most resounding activities of the International were purely declaratory – and few of its pronouncements were unaccompanied by jarring discords. Even those organizations which vociferated with the majority at congresses were in their everyday activity preoccupied with local issues and guided by local tactical considerations.

Both Blanquists and Bakuninists felt that Marxist insistence on the struggle for power within existing social institutions blunted the revolutionary urge. There was force in this criticism. Marx's critics could have added that political activity in the Marxist sense narrowed the vision of working class organization to the national scene. Marx himself found that his English trade unionist friends were too absorbed in the struggle for electoral reform – of which in itself he naturally approved – and that many of them grew more and more parochial when alliance with the liberals seemed likely to satisfy their demands. Interest in the International, ironically, waned wherever working-class organization gained self-assurance in the national political context. It was, after all, no more than a pious assumption that the working class at large was actually, or potentially, internationalist in outlook. The dissidents who tried to force through the 1867 congress a resolution restricting membership to manual workers and excluding brain workers would surely have had even more difficulty than Marx and the General Council in maintaining a coherent international movement. As working-class organizations grew stronger their leaders were naturally more concerned with the immediate needs and interests of their supporters, and less in need of psychological reassurance from a supranational body.

Marx decided in the early 1870s that the first drive towards international unification had lost impetus, and that the attempt could only be profitably renewed when strong working-class parties were firmly established in a number of countries. If he had failed as an organizer his success as propagandist and educator was enormous. The quest for unity would be resumed by political parties most of which acknowledged him as their ideological only true begetter.

4

The Second International: Orthodoxy and Heresy

On 14 July 1889, the hundredth anniversary of the fall of the Bastille, representatives of working class and socialist organizations from twenty countries met in Paris to establish the Second International. Engels had at first doubted the timeliness of this step, but German and French Marxists hastened to seize the initiative from a band of reformist socialists and trade unionists who gathered in Paris simultaneously. In the early years the anarchists tried to reopen their battle with 'state socialism' within the Second International, but in 1896 after a series of hot skirmishes they were expelled. At successive congresses the International resolved that economic and political struggle must always be combined, that socialists everywhere must fight for universal suffrage to increase the political weight of the working class, and that only organizations committed to political activity should be admitted to its ranks. As immediate practical measures for sealing international solidarity the working class in all countries was urged to observe May Day as a proletarian holiday, and to campaign for the eight-hour working day. In short, the Marxist programme of political struggle within the existing social order became the declared policy of the International.

The dominant parties, like Marx in his time, professed to see revolution as the ultimate aim, and the day-to-day struggle of parliamentary parties and trades unions as a necessary preparatory stage. Engels in 1893 reminded his flock that the final emancipation of the working class was impossible without violent revolution, and his friend, Karl Kautsky, who after 1895 succeeded him as the 'socialist Pope' (though Marx had thought him muddle-headed Philistine), went on talking periodically about revolution. None the less, the International did not make Marxist orthodoxy, or a declaration of revolutionary intent, conditions of membership. A vaguely worded resolution of 1896 authorized all methods of political struggle, and in 1908 the 'more Methodist than

24

Marxist' British Labour Party could be admitted with only faint noises of disgust from the left. The Second International was essentially a consultative body, and until the International Socialist Bureau was set up in 1900 it had no forum for regular discussions between congresses. A central directorate with the pretensions of Marx's General Council would soon have wrecked this loose association of autonomous groups, each with its distinctive ideological tinge and its peculiar local problems. Their diversity sometimes made necessary tactfully vague statements of policy, and such resolutions as that of the London Congress (1896) on the agrarian problem, or that of the Paris Congress (1900) on the participation of socialists in bourgeois governments, in effect authorized member parties to do as they liked without Marxist qualms. In any case it was tacitly accepted that decisions of the International were not mandatory and had only moral force.

At congresses of the International the German Social Democratic Party enjoyed greater respect and authority than any other. It owed its pre-eminence to its size, its formal unity, the discipline and efficiency of its local organizational machinery, the prestige of its theorists, and above all to its electoral strength. Between 1890, when it was legalized, and 1912 the Party's membership grew from 100,000 to 1 million. On the eve of the First World War Social Democrats held a quarter of the seats in the Reichstag. But the Reichstag, as the French Socialist Jaurès once sharply reminded his German comrades, was not a real parliament. In Imperial Germany the Social Democrats were at best a tolerated nuisance, and the Kaiser's government hampered their activities by all means possible. In its official pronouncements the Party was often at pains not to provoke the wrath of the All Highest. Thus the programme adopted at Erfurt in 1891 (and superseded only in 1921) spoke not of revolution but of 'the collapse of capitalism', and (to Engels's annoyance) did not include dictatorship of the proletariat, or even a democratic republic, among the Party's declared aims. It was impossible, for fear of official interference and reprisals against the SPD, to hold a congress of the International in Germany until 1907.

Worse still, the unity of the Party was more specious than real. The South Germans showed considerable independence both in their drive for the electoral support of the peasantry, and in their tactical local alliances with liberal groups. More important were the ideological fissures caused by the tensions of political struggle

25

in an authoritarian state. The lines of cleavage along which the Party would split under the strain of the First World War were already discernible around 1900. The most searching criticism of the Party's official creed came from Eduard Bernstein, who had spent some years in London and was impressed by the potentialities of Fabian tactics in English circumstances. He argued that orthodox Marxism in some important respects no longer corresponded to observable realities. In particular, Marx had underestimated the vitality of capitalism. Modern credit policies and cartelization had made crises of overproduction less frequent and less acute. The working class was becoming more prosperous, not steadily poorer as Marx expected. The trend towards fuller democracy in the capitalist countries made it possible for the working class to achieve more and more of its aspirations by peaceful means. Talk of revolution was pointless, unless what was meant was simply radical change. The SPD should 'dare to appear what in fact it is – a democratic socialist party of reform', and should systematically apply the pressures of its parliamentary strength, the trades unions and the co-operative movement to improving the condition of the working class.

The repercussions of Bernstein's 'revisionism' spread throughout the International. Not surprisingly, socialists from backward countries were among Bernstein's hottest critics. The Tsarist Empire, in particular, was half a century or more behind Western Europe in economic development, and Marx's analysis had lost none of its actuality for such as Georgi Plekhanov, who instilled Marxist thought into Russian Socialism, or Lenin or the Polish Socialist Rosa Luxemburg. Moreover, until 1905 the Tsarist autocracy tolerated neither political parties nor independent trade unions, so that a reformist programme could hold little attraction for Russian or Polish socialists.

The reactions of the German socialist leaders were much less sharply defined. In its practice, the Party was reformist through and through, and avoided actions or, as a rule, official pronouncements which its best friends, or worst enemies, could call revolutionary. But the leaders were not tempted to jettison any part of their Marxist heritage. Many of them could have said with Bernstein that 'the movement is everything – the end nothing'. Yet even for Bernstein the end, though vaguer than Marx's vision of revolutionary proletarian dictatorship, was a 'substantial change' transcending immediate small gains. Not surprisingly, some of his colleagues felt that open revision could only sap the militancy of the Party even in its day-to-day activities. Hence the rebuke, cynical or merely naive, which Ignaz Auer, a member of the Party presidium addressed to Bernstein: 'One does not say these things – one just does them.'

The decisive consideration for all Social Democrats was the unity of the Party. Many of its low level activists and rank and file members were spontaneous reformists, while much of its electoral support would have been frightened away by a genuine revolutionary stance. Unity demanded a tactful blurring of ideology. For the dominant faction in the leadership, it was enough to preserve revolution as a theoretical ultima ratio, a vague threat for the future which the bourgeoisie would hasten to forestall by concessions in the present. Uneasier Marxist consciences, like that of Kautsky or Rosa Luxemburg, could find some relief in speculation on the new social and economic trends which would sooner or later revolutionize the masses and 'their' Party. Rosa's insistence that day-to-day activities should always be adjusted to the ultimate revolutionary aim was almost as embarrassing to the leadership as Bernstein's open revisionism. Yet although she and her friends were an isolated minority on the far left of the Party she had no thought before 1914 of splitting it; she thought of the Party as a machine to be kept intact and strong for eventual use by the masses: and she cherished a pathetic belief that with or without the consent of the Auers the masses would at last use it in a revolutionary way.

In France no formula, and no organization, could hide the differences between orthodox Marxists (particularly the Parti Ouvrier of Jules Guesde) on the one hand, and the impatient proletarians who in 1895 came together in the powerful *Confédération Générale du Travail*. The syndicalists were intolerant of parliamentary delays, of the compromises inevitable in a democratic process of reform. They believed in 'direct action' by the workers to improve their lot, which included the conclusion of labour contracts, but also on occasion sabotage, in a variety of forms: the go-slow, work to rule, deliberately bad work, wrecking and above all strike action, with, as its ultimate aim, the general strike to overthrow the bourgeoisie. Ideologists of syndicalism, principally Georges Sorel, looked to the trades unions as the future organizers of society, once the exploiting bourgeoisie and the whole apparatus of its state had been brought down in ruins.

Sorel, with his savage contempt for parliamentary Marxism and for socialist intellectuals, whom he regarded as infinitely cowardly and corruptible, claimed to be restoring the healthy nucleus of Marxism: its exaltation of class struggle. The example of Millerand, whose accession to a coalition government was lengthily and inconclusively debated by the Second International, should show the workers that they could expect nothing from politicians who called themselves socialist. Sorel worried about the flabby degeneration of the bourgeoisie, ever more willing to buy peace with minor concessions, as well as about the seductive illusions of social democracy. A vicious bourgeoisie was necessary to the morale of the revolutionary worker, and Sorel urged spontaneous violence as a means of putting fresh life into the class struggle. At the end of his days, not surprisingly, he found something to admire both in Lenin and in Mussolini.

The idea of the general strike had a long history. In the 1840s Robert Owen had seen it as the irresistible weapon of his proposed Grand National Trade Union, embracing all the workers of Britain and fusing their demands in a single ultimatum. The Brussels Congress of the First International (1868) had favoured it as means of preventing war. It was taken up with enthusiasm by the Bakuninists, and fiercely criticized by Marx and Engels, who held in horror all ideas tending to divorce 'economic' from 'political' struggle. Early in the twentieth century, however, impatient workers in many countries felt that the 'political struggle' served the needs of careerist intellectuals rather than their own. Even in Britain the great strikes of 1911 (seamen, dockers and railwaymen) and 1912 (miners), and the formation of the 'Triple Industrial Alliance' (miners, railwaymen and transport workers) in 1913, owed something to the influence of French syndicalism, imported by Ben Tillet and Tom Mann (the leaders of the revolutionary strikes of 1889) from Australia. Within the fortress of 'orthodox' Marxism itself, the Second International, the general strike began again to seem a feasible means of checking governments bent on war.

Neither reformism nor revolutionary syndicalism had much relevance in backward autocratic Russia, which lacked even the sketchiest parliamentary institutions until 1906, and where before the 1905 Revolution the only trade unions were welfare associations run by the Ministry of the Interior. There were, it is true, Russian Marxists who believed that the workers should concentrate for the present on their 'economic' demands and ignore politics (the 'Economists'), and others who believed that they could as yet contribute nothing to Russia's political development except by way of propaganda and education (the 'Legal Marxists'). But inevitably, the strongest trend in Russian social democracy was uncompromisingly 'political' and revolutionary. The events of 1905 made the hitherto obscure, and chronically divided, Russian Social Democratic Party a force to be reckoned with in the international movement.

5

The Russian Revolution of 1905

Since the mid-nineteenth century Imperial Russia had been fitfully at grips with a problem which it finally proved incapable of solving: that of accommodating rapid economic modernization within the institutional framework of an uncompromising autocracy. The Great Reforms of the 1860s – the emancipation of the serfs, the establishment of open courts with an independent judiciary, the creation of elected local government bodies (*zemstva*) the easing of censorship and the concession of a measure of autonomy to universities – had stimulated liberal hopes that political reform would go hand in hand with economic development. But, as so often, limited concessions provoked further demands, and a relatively conciliatory government which resisted liberal appeals suddenly found itself confronted with a powerful revolutionary challenge. Marx and Engels considered the Russian populists of the 1860s and 1870s ideologically naive and 'unscientific', but admired enormously their revolutionary ardour and self-sacrificing fanaticism. In 1879–81 populist terrorists seemed to have brought the autocracy to bay. For the first time since the disappointing episode of the Paris Commune, which had come after two decades of stagnation in the European revolutionary movement, there seemed to be a lively hope that one reactionary government would be overthrown. And for Marx and Engels Russia was the main bulwark of international reaction. Hence their readiness to slur over their ideological doubts about populism, and to concede that agrarian revolution in Russia might lead to the establishment of socialism based on the peasant commune, as proposed by the populists, if it set in train proletarian revolutions elsewhere. Even the terrorist conspiratorial methods of the People's Will Party, which in 1881 succeeded in assassinating Tsar Alexander II, were temporarily acceptable. If ever the Blanquist fantasy had any chance of realization, said Engels later, it was in Russia in 1881.

In fact, the Tsar's 'execution' was the despairing act of a dwindling and beleaguered group. People's Will succeeded only in nerving the Tsarist government to stamp out conspiracy, repress even the most pacific liberal demands, retract as much as possible of the concessions made under Alexander II and 'freeze Russia lest it go rotten'. In the next two decades the population grew with unprecedented rapidity, the railway network expanded, new industries sprang up. But the government, even after the great famine of 1891–2, did little or nothing to appease the land-hunger of the peasantry, while placing squarely on them the fiscal burden of financing industrial growth. Minor measures to ease the hardships of the workers densely packed in the slums or factory barracks of older industrial areas, or in the shanty towns of the Ukrainian coal basin and the Baku oilfields, were not enforced in practice. The condition of the Russian working class in 1900 was in many respects like that of its Western counterparts in the early nineteenth century: and no quick improvement could be expected from a government which saw the abundance of cheap labour as Russia's main economic advantage.

Dissenting liberals had strongholds in the *zemstva* (and particularly amongst the specialists employed in local government agencies), the universities and the free professions, but their representatives were rebuffed by Nicholas II on his accession in 1894, and although they held clandestine conferences earlier they had no opportunity to voice their aspirations openly until 1904. An abortive conspiracy against the life of Alexander III in 1887, for which Lenin's older brother Alexander Ulyanov was hanged, marked the demise of the People's Will Party. Thereafter, and until the turn of the century, the forces of the revolutionary movement were scattered about various places of confinement and banishment in the Russian Empire, and the cities of Western Europe. The first Russian Marxist Party, the League for the Liberation of Labour, was formed by three self-critical ex-populists, Plekhanov, Axelrod and Vera Zasulich, in 1883: but its following even amongst émigrés remained tiny, and its only important activity was the dissemination of Plekhanov's writings. Inside Russia sporadic socialist study groups, often of a semi-populist, semi-Marxist complexion, seldom escaped police vigilance for more than a few months at a time. The young Lenin in St Petersburg in the mid-1890s found the nascent workers' groups wary of compromising contact with agitators from outside. The

Russian Social Democratic Party founded in Minsk in 1898, after Lenin's banishment to Shushenskoye was, to begin with, a grandiose label for a tiny group of intellectuals, most of whom were arrested soon after.

In the first few years of the twentieth century the Tsarist regime suddenly found the dykes of authoritarian immobilism crumbling under the pent-up pressure of the people's resentment. The most destructive jacqueries in modern Russian history swept through the central Black Earth and middle Volga provinces in 1902–4, as desperate peasants seized land, cattle and crops from the gentry and burnt their manor houses. In 1902 a massive strike broke out in the Baku oilfields, where Joseph Dzhugashvili (Stalin) was among the most active agitators: and the strikers put forward political as well as economic demands. The new Socialist Revolutionary Party, founded in 1901 and claiming descent from People's Will, won considerable support amongst the restive peasants, and in an escalating terrorist campaign numbered one minister of education, two ministers of the interior, a powerful uncle of the Tsar and several provincial governors among its victims. To head off the forces of revolution, the government set up an elaborate network of committees to report on the needs of agriculture, and experimented with workers' organizations under police management (the Zubatov unions). But its main hopes were placed on more efficient repression, and, shortly, on a weird recipe for reconciliation between Tsar and people proposed by Vyacheslav Plehve, Minister of the Interior: a little victorious war. Japan, the enemy cast by Plehve as Tsardom's saviour, attacked Port Arthur without declaring war in January 1904. The series of catastrophic defeats which Russia suffered in the next fifteen months, and the progressive disorganization of the country, almost brought the autocratic system down in ruins.

The disorders of 1902–4 and the floundering of the government had energized and emboldened liberal opposition, amongst whom the militant left, with its demands for a legislative assembly, and its readiness to consider joint action with revolutionaries in order to break the government's resistance, quickly became dominant. After Plehve's assassination in July 1904 the Tsar adopted conciliatory tactics, and two successive ministers of the interior worked on minimal concessions to be introduced with the maximum delay.

The massacre on Bloody Sunday (22 January 1905) forced the

pace of events. Troops opened fire on a procession of workers bearing a petition to the Tsar, led by Father Gapon, a priest who had earlier organized a 'Zubatov union' under police supervision. Perhaps a thousand demonstrators were killed and several thousand wounded. A wave of strikes and mass demonstrations raced across the country, and the government completely lost control and credibility. Sympathetic or circumspect employers often continued paying workers out on strike. The middle class at large, and even the lower levels of the administration, ignored appeals and orders from on high. The revolution was spontaneous and unco-ordinated, but in mid-summer the liberal left with its call for a Constituent Assembly gave a focus for popular demands. In August the Tsar's decision to set up a consultative assembly (duma), and the conclusion of peace with Japan on lenient but still humiliating terms, did nothing to restore the government's credit. The strike movement faltered briefly in summer, but regained impetus and reached its climax in October, when the railwaymen and telegraphists came out, in effect severing communications between the government and the country at large. The stubborn Tsar's first thought was to appoint a military dictator, but the Grand Duke whom he approached threatened to commit suicide unless he bowed instead to the nation's demands. On 30 October the Tsar promulgated a Manifesto promising civic freedoms, the eventual extension of the franchise to all classes and the creation of a Duma with powers to approve or reject all legislative proposals and supervise the legality of government actions.

When the Revolution of 1905 broke out Russian Social Democrats were taken by surprise. Most of their leaders, indeed, were in exile at the beginning of the year – and Lenin reached Russia only in November. 1905 swelled the ranks of the revolutionary parties and gave them their baptism of fire. But though Socialist Revolutionaries and Social Democrats gained footholds amongst the workers and peasants they were too weak to impose cohesion and unity of purpose on what was essentially a spontaneous mass revolt. For the Social Democrats the main scene of activity since 1900 had been in Western Europe, where émigré intellectuals intrigued and squabbled for control over the nascent party and its press. In 1903 the Party had split into two factions – Bolsheviks ('majority men') and Mensheviks ('minority men'). These appellations were fortuitously acquired as the result of a vote at an unrepresentative meeting where, with his usual opportunistic and propagandistic flair, Lenin snatched the title, Bolsheviks, for his distinctly minority faction. Nominally, they were divided only by different opinions as to the qualifications for Party membership: the Mensheviks favouring a broad definition which would draw in sympathizers as well as professional revolutionaries, the Bolsheviks insisting that all members must participate actively in the work of a party organization.

It shortly became clear, however, that this apparently minor difference was symptomatic of a much wider and deeper division between the two groups. The Mensheviks remained committed to what they regarded as the classical Marxist scheme, of a two-stage revolution: the liberal bourgeoisie must first set up a democratic republic, within which the working class, enfranchised and free to organize itself, would eventually carry out its own revolution for the introduction of socialism. Lenin's reaction to this was not unlike that of Tkachev to Marx. He saw no sense in postponing the revolution for socialism to an indefinite future, and in the meantime harnessing the workers' movement to the rickety chariot of the Russian middle class. He did not deny that bourgeois democratic freedom must be the immediate aim for the workers too: but their natural allies at this stage were the peasant mass, not the liberal bourgeoisie. In the late 1890s, by laborious and ingenious statistical analysis, Lenin had convinced himself that a process of polarization among the Russian peasantry was already well advanced. It was a short step to the conclusion that the proletariat, after winning bourgeois freedom in alliance with the peasantry at large, would quickly find in the poor and 'middle' peasants allies for the next, socialist stage of the revolution. Heretical as it seemed to the Mensheviks, Lenin's programme can reasonably be regarded as a Russian variant of the 'permanent revolution' envisaged by Marx in 1850. Only a tightly disciplined party of professional organizers could effectively manipulate a fluid 'permanently revolutionary' situation: and the Leninist concept of the Party is often traced to the Jacobin populist Tkachev rather than to Marx.

Russian conditions in fact compelled the Mensheviks also to behave as a conspiratorial elite: but their major tasks, as they saw it, lay ahead in a bourgeois democratic Russia, and their ideal socialist party naturally owed more to contemporary German example than to Russian revolutionary tradition.

In 1905, Lenin called for an armed uprising of workers and

peasants to establish a provisional revolutionary government in which – to the scandal of the Mensheviks – he recommended social democratic participation. In practice, the rush and confusion of events flung Bolsheviks, Mensheviks and even Socialist Revolutionaries (SRs) who envisaged the peasantry and the commune as the centre of a new agrarian socialism, together in uneasy alliances and concerted limited action. Towards the end of the year, the Mensheviks in St Petersburg and the Bolsheviks in Moscow suffered heavy defeats. In June, the textile workers of Ivanovo-Voznesensk had elected a delegate assembly to co-ordinate their activity. Similar bodies, which came to be called 'Soviets', sprang up in fifty or so other centres. The most impressive of them was the St Petersburg Soviet, formed on 13 October, with delegates from 181 places of work and 16 trades unions. The Soviet provided a platform for the fiery rhetoric of Trotsky (then nominally a Menshevik) who became chairman late in November. For six weeks or so the Soviet thundered its support of extreme liberal demands, issued decrees on labour conditions and municipal affairs, published its own newspaper. However, the Menshevik group made no preparations for an armed uprising, and could make no resistance when the police dispersed the Soviet and arrested its leaders on 16 December.

Bolshevik hopes of a revolution in arms were inflamed by the massive Lodz uprising in June, which found echoes throughout the Empire; and also by signs of disaffection in the armed forces, such as the mutiny on the battleship Potemkin in August. The 'Technical Group' of the Bolshevik Central Committee, under L. B. Krasin, bought arms in Russia and abroad, set up workshops to make explosives, encouraged local party committees to form fighting squads and sent agitators to restless military units. Lenin urged the Soviets to see themselves not only as the nuclei of future proletarian government but as the organizers of armed revolt. In December, disorders among garrison troops, and a railway strike which temporarily halted traffic into the city, emboldened the Bolsheviks in the Moscow Soviet to summon the population to arms. Barricades were thrown up. The Governor General declared a state of emergency. Street battles raged for ten days (20–30 December) until reliable troops were brought in from St Petersburg and Warsaw. The rising was finally shattered by artillery bombardment of the working-class district of Presnya. Over 1,000 people perished in the fighting, and the Governor General regretted that the quick collapse of the rising prevented extermination of the rebels. Throughout December and into the new year sporadic risings occurred in the Baltic provinces, the Ukraine, South Russia, the Caucasus and Siberia, and the first 'Soviet republics' arose in areas temporarily inaccessible to the Tsar's troops.

Plekhanov, speaking for most Mensheviks, declared the uprisings a grievous error. But for Lenin they were the high-point of what he came to call the 'dress rehearsal'. The Russian people, previously 'incapable of large-scale armed struggle with the exploiters', was now battle-hardened, and in the Soviets and the fighting squads had created organizational forms which a future revolution would adopt and perfect.

The Bolsheviks had need of such consolations in the next few years, as the revolutionary wave ebbed. Exhausted by the upheavals of late 1905 the workers hopefully contemplated the mirage conjured up by the Tsar: thereafter, a new industrial boom, rising wages, legalized if feeble trades unions and the beginnings of welfare legislation steadily reduced their militancy. In the first two Dumas the anti-governmental majority regarded themselves as the advance guard of an embattled nation, pursuing the aims of the revolution by parliamentary means, and ready to raise the people up against the government should it prove recalcitrant. But the Tsar dismissed these assemblies without popular protest, and a new electoral law promulgated unconstitutionally in June 1907 enabled Prime Minister Pyotr Stolypin to reach a *modus vivendi* with the Third Duma. Some of the peasants' rankling grievances had received quick attention: in particular, redemption payments for peasant land were abolished in December 1906. Stolypin introduced legislation to assist peasant land purchase and large-scale resettlement from overpopulated areas to Siberia and Central Asia. More important, he sought to convert the 'stronger' peasants into a class of conservative smallholders by enabling them to leave the commune and consolidate their holdings in private farms. Lenin was among those who thought that such policies might indeed change the balance of social forces: he gloomily foresaw the possibility that ties between the proletariat and the peasantry at large might be severed, and that only landless rural proletarians would readily ally themselves with the workers. His pessimism was heightened by the success of Stolypin's repressive measures: between August 1906 and April 1907 1,102 persons accused of subversive activity were summarily tried and executed by military field-courts, and the Prime Minister remained impervious to protests against 'Stolypin's necktie' in the Duma and abroad, where Ramsay MacDonald, for instance, denounced the Tsar as a 'common murderer'. Vigorous police action dispersed and immobilized revolutionary groups. Until 1917 for most professional social democrat revolutionaries political activity meant mainly factional squabbling in emigration, or improving their political education in Siberia.

Stolypin's plans for converting Russia into an economically strong bourgeois monarchy presupposed a long period of peace, and his independence of mind soon earned him the detestation of powerful reactionary circles, including the Tsar himself. In September 1911 he was assassinated by an ambiguous creature who might have emerged from the pages of Conrad's *Under Western Eyes*: a petty revolutionary dreamer and schemer who had drifted into the employ of the secret police. It is possible that the murder was officially instigated. The Tsar took care not to appoint a strong successor, and lost sight of the need to keep Russia at all costs out of the European war which, during the Balkan turmoil of 1912–13, already seemed at hand. Lenin, who had clung to the idea of a second armed uprising in 1906–7, and ever since had professed to regard it as only briefly postponed, was encouraged by a mounting strike wave in 1912–13. But his great hope lay in the shattering effect which he confidently expected a major war to have on the ramshackle Russian Empire. A 'revolutionary defeatist' during the Russo–Japanese war, Lenin was equally indifferent in 1914 to the prospect of Russia's defeat by another 'more advanced' country, Imperial Germany. His one anxiety, expressed in a letter to Gorky, was that 'Franz Joseph and Nikolasha [the Tsar] won't do us the favour'.

Lenin also cherished illusions about the immediate reactions of the masses in Europe, and of the working-class parties, to the outbreak of war. Russian social democrats, after the 1905 Revolution, had enjoyed a prominence within the councils of the Second International out of all proportion to their importance at home, or the relevance of their ideas to Western parties. The 'general strike' as the organizational framework of a national revolution commanded much support amongst German and French socialists after 1905, and a somewhat idealized conception of 'Soviets' already supplied a model for future imitation. The Bolsheviks, it is true, were dissatisfied with the International's efforts to mediate between rival groups of Russian social democrats: such pundits as Kautsky never fully fathomed their ideological differences, justifiably suspecting that Lenin's will to power aggravated them, and on the whole preferred the Mensheviks. None the less, both Lenin, the Bolshevik, and Plekhanov and Martov the Mensheviks, carried considerable weight in the International, and used it effectively at one stage to influence thinking on the policy of socialist parties in the event of war.

6

The Second International and the War of 1914

In the early years of the century, as friction between the European powers increased, resolutions deploring war ceased to satisfy many socialists and they pressed for concerted action to avert it. The main immediate sources of tension were the scramble for colonies and markets and rivalry between Austria and Russia in the Balkans: but each successive crisis, whatever its origin, inflamed French fear and resentment of Germany, and Germany's desire to consolidate the victory of 1870. The sealing of the Triple Entente in 1906–7 (although the anxious Russians thought it an elusive 'sea serpent' of an alliance) brought the threat of war between the two countries closer. It was natural, therefore, that the liveliest dialogue on joint measures against war should be between French and German socialists. At the Seventh Congress of the International at Stuttgart in 1907 measures to prevent war were the main business on the agenda. The debate brought out sharply a long discernible difference in their attitudes, and the argument between them became, ironically, a fight for supremacy within the International. The French socialists had never achieved the specious solidarity of their German comrades, and the majority group of Jaurès made no pretence of Marxist orthodoxy. Their proposals were, none the less, far more militant and concrete than those of the notionally united and orthodox Germans. In particular, Jaurès amongst others, urged that the hand of any would-be belligerent government should be stayed by a general strike. The doubts of working class leaders about the feasibility of such an action are easily understood, but it is also true that no critic of the French resolution, and least of all the German socialist leadership, had a comparably concrete proposal.

The issue was passed to a sub-commission, and it was here that a formula of immense historical significance was evolved. The successful compromise resolution included an amendment drafted by Lenin, Martov and Rosa Luxemburg to the effect that if (in spite of the efforts of socialists)

> War should nevertheless break out, it is their duty to intervene to bring it to an end at once and to make the fullest use of the economic and political crisis created by the war in order to stir up the deepest strata of the people and hasten the collapse of capitalist domination.

The resolution satisfied the Germans by omitting any mention of general strike, appeased the French with its militant verbiage and in effect prescribed revolution as the means of smothering war. It seems unlikely that most of those who voted for this resolution saw it as more than a rhetorical threat to governments. Their intention was perhaps more accurately reflected in the awful warning uttered by the Basle Congress in 1912:

> The workers regard it as a crime to shoot at each other for the sake of capitalist profits, dynastic pride, or deals concluded in secret treaties. If governments, suppressing all possibility of normal evolution, drive the proletariat of all Europe to desperate resolves, it is they who will bear full responsibility for the crisis provoked by them.

However this may be, no further progress was made at the congresses of Copenhagen (1910) and Basle (1912), nor in the animated consultations organized by the International Socialist Bureau, towards a more precise definition of the practical forms which opposition to war might take.

The assassination of Jaurès on 31 July 1914 seemed to symbolize the helplessness of socialists everywhere in face of rampant chauvinism. Four days later, the behaviour of the German Social Democratic deputies in the Reichstag revealed how feeble was the spirit of internationalism in this most Marxist of parties. With only one abstention they voted for the granting of war credits to the Imperial government. The full import of this act can only be realized if we remember that in peace-time Social Democrats had habitually voted against the government's budget proposals as a routine gesture of protest against the existing political order. Their action in 1914 has been depicted as the first of a series of 'betrayals' which fatally weakened German social democracy, and led even, in the view of some writers, directly to the rise of Nazism and the Second World War. More certainly, it accelerated a profound and enduring split between reformist and revolutionary Marxists. In reality, this was a polarization of opposing tendencies in Marxism itself. If the SPD leaders 'betrayed' in 1914, then had they not been traitors for a quarter of a century past? They had never clearly seen, and Marxism had not helped them to see, at what point they should abandon political activity within the existing framework for revolution. Should they in 1914 have defied the sentiment of the German masses, imperilled the substantial position which they had won in the German political system, set themselves up in opposition not merely to the government but to most of their supporters? Or should they continue to use this drastically changed political situation to build up their own strength by the old familiar political methods. As usual, the Party was not unanimous as to what the methods should be. A centrist group, which gained strength as the war went on, favoured neither all-out support for the war, nor revolutionary opposition. This division eroded the unity of the parliamentary faction, and the number of social-democratic abstentions from subsequent votes on war credits grew. Even so, the fetish of party unity held the SPD together until April 1917, when the centrists broke away to form the Independent Social Democratic Party (USPD). And even then, the extremist anti-war faction, led by Rosa Luxemburg and Karl Liebknecht, remained uneasily within this new party of judicious non-co-operators until the war had run its course. Only a small splinter group at Bremen made a clean break with both sections of the old leadership.

The behaviour of socialists in other parliaments resembled that of the SPD. In all Europe only two Serbian socialist deputies, and the tiny Bolshevik and Menshevik groups in the Russian Duma, condemned the war from the start. Elsewhere, even non-co-operating socialists and conscientious objectors assumed, like Kautsky, that political struggle was suspended for the duration. A commoner attitude was 'defensism' – the argument that defence of working-class interests must include defence of the fatherland. All the belligerents of course claimed to be fighting a war of self-defence, and socialists everywhere found good reasons for identifying themselves with the national cause. The Austrian leader, Victor Adler, thought it hopeless to swim against the tide of popular patriotism. Ancient fears and prejudices assured the German defensists that resistance to tyrannical and barbarous Russia must be in the interests of progress. The dominant groups in the French Socialist Party and the British trade union movement were just as passionately convinced that their countries were threatened by a ruthlessly aggressive Germany. In Germany, some socialist leaders acted as intermediaries between the government and the working class, while in France and Britain a few socialists took ministerial office. Even amongst the Russians Plekhanov, most Mensheviks, and most Socialist Revolutionaries, temporarily abandoned the struggle with Tsardom and struck a patriotic pose.

7

Lenin and the War

Lenin was almost the only socialist of international renown who from the start welcomed the war as the midwife of revolution. As soon as Franz Joseph and Nikolasha after all 'obliged', and Lenin (with the help of the Austrian 'opportunist' and 'social patriot' Victor Adler) made his way from Galicia to Switzerland, he set about the task of rescuing what little was left of revolutionary Marxism from the wreckage of the Second International, and preparing to exploit the revolutionary opportunities which the war would create.

In a declaration of the 'Central Committee of the Russian Social Democratic Workers' Party' dated 28 October 1914 Lenin, invoking the memory of the Paris Commune and the resolution of the Basle Congress, called on the workers everywhere to 'turn the present imperialist war into civil war', and to create a new 'proletarian International, liberated from opportunism'. He sought in vain to win the support of left-wing dissidents in other parties for these policies at two international conferences, held at Zimmerwald in September 1915 and Kienthal in April 1916. At Zimmerwald, the majority (including delegates from Rosa Luxemburg's group) would accept only a resolution condemning Social Democrats who supported the war and urging the working class to fight for a peace without annexations. The Kienthal conference produced only a feeble appeal to socialists to stop supporting belligerent governments, and to vote against war credits. Though the Third International would later trace its origins to the 'Zimmerwald left', the anti-war groups in Western parties showed no inclination to follow Russian leadership before the October Revolution. The prevalent attitude was that of Rosa Luxemburg, who admired Lenin's fire and intellectual power, but disliked his authoritarianism and feared the results of a premature seizure of power in a backward country.

Lenin sometimes found it hard to keep his revolutionary optimism alive during the war. He was very ready to believe rumours that Germany and Russia were seeking to patch up a separate peace. Disappointed by the quiescence of the masses in the warring countries he found some consolation in growing governmental intervention in the economy, which could facilitate transition to socialism via state capitalism. His frustration vented itself in furious attacks on the collaborating social patriots and vacillating centrists in the workers' parties. More and more, his hopes were concentrated on Russia's defeat as the lesser evil for the European working class, and the dawn of new opportunities. On the eve of the Tsar's overthrow he spoke in a Swiss gathering of socialism as a distant prospect.

8

The Russian Revolutions of 1917

The collapse of Tsarism in February 1917 took Lenin by surprise, as well it might. It was not a mighty revolutionary blow, but the huffs of a handful of liberal politicians which crumpled the autocracy. They seized the occasion of unrest in Petrograd, caused by food shortages and the indiscipline of battle-shy troops, to set up a Provisional Government and force the Tsar to abdicate. They were able to do so because the Tsar's absence at the front, and the confusing division of powers between the military and civil authorities, had disorganized the government, and because the generals felt that the removal of the hapless Supreme Commander would help them to conduct the war more efficiently. They looked to the liberal politicians to restore the nation's morale, disastrously damaged by the defeats and hardships of 1916–17, and to stabilize the home front. But the government's position was precarious. Self-appointed and unrepresentative, it inaugurated what Lenin himself called a period of unprecedented freedom. Amongst other things it lifted restrictions on political activity, released political prisoners and allowed exiled revolutionaries to return. The calculation of P. N. Milyukov and A. I. Guchkov, the strongest personalities in the First Provisional Government, was that the country would rally to defend the gains and promises of the February 'revolution'. When in April it became clear that they identified this concept with 'war to final victory' they were forced to resign by an outcry from the left, and from then on the Provisional Government was dominated by the ex-Socialist Revolutionary Alexander Kerensky, a virtuoso of ultra-democratic rhetoric with little political sense or organizing ability, who succeeded Guchkov at the War Ministry and became Prime Minister in July.

The Provisional Government depended for its survival on the acquiescence of a more broadly based centre of authority: the Petrograd Soviet of Workers' and Soldiers' Deputies. This uneasy 'duality of power', as Trotsky called it, could have been quickly resolved by a Soviet coup. But the Mensheviks and Socialist Revolutionaries who dominated the Soviet shirked responsibility for the conduct of affairs while the war lasted, and particularly for the unpopular measures which it must make necessary. The Mensheviks could plead their well-known belief that a period of bourgeois democracy must precede the assumption of power by the people, and most SRs were glad to join them in this flimsy ideological shelter. While refusing to rule themselves, they seriously undermined the authority of the Provisional Government. Order No. 1 of the Soviet Executive Committee advised soldiers to obey only those commands which did not conflict with the instructions of the Soviet, and to elect in every unit committees which would co-operate with that body. The resultant erosion of discipline in the army was largely responsible for the failure of the Galician campaign in July, by which Kerensky had hoped to obtain a breathing space and possibly peace with the Central Powers.

The Bolsheviks in Petrograd, including Stalin (but with Molotov demurring), had at first called not for the overthrow of the Provisional Government but for pressure on it to negotiate peace. In mid-April they were jolted into militancy by the arrival of Lenin, whose return from Switzerland together with other left-wing émigrés was arranged by the Germans on the sound calculation that they would aggravate the confusion inside Russia. Lenin chided his faint-hearted colleagues, called for the withdrawal of all support from the government, the transfer of power to the Soviets, the overthrow of capitalism and the termination of the imperialist war. Lenin's 'April Theses' were ridiculed by the other socialist parties, and some of his followers saw little point in pressing power on their reluctant rivals. He had, however, judged the situation shrewdly. The rise of Kerensky, who represented himself as the watchdog of the Soviets in the government, and the acceptance of ministries by other socialists in May, reduced friction between the two centres of power, but also frayed the bonds between the large socialist parties and a people craving peace and reform. In early summer peasants began seizing land, ignoring the government's pleas for patience. Land seizures accelerated desertion from the army, as soldiers rushed to make sure of their share. Lenin could realistically expect that the masses would listen more and more readily to the one party which promised quick gratification of their demands.

Rioting in Petrograd on 16 and 17 July was set off by news of the Galician débâcle. Bolshevik banners were prominent in street demonstrations, and mutinous troops took up the slogan 'All Power to the Soviets!' Growing incomprehension among the masses of the official Soviet position was pithily expressed by a worker who demanded of the Socialist Revolutionary Chernov, who served as Minister of Agriculture in the Provisional government: 'Why won't you take power when it's offered, sons of bitches?' The Soviet leaders retorted by publishing allegations that Lenin was a paid agent of the German government, arresting two Bolshevik leaders, and banning the Bolshevik newspaper *Pravda*. Lenin went into hiding, and spent his time writing *State and Revolution*, a Utopian tract intended to show that, contrary to the views of some of his nearest colleagues, as well as of the Mensheviks, the Russian people was ripe for proletarian democracy.

The 'July days' were a grave setback to the Bolsheviks, but an improbable rescuer was at hand. Kerensky had sought to restore discipline in the army, and to bolster the government's tottering power, in alliance with the new, efficient and ambitious commander-in-chief, General L. G. Kornilov. When, however, Kornilov sent troops to Petrograd in September ostensibly to help keep order, Kerensky took fright and summoned the left to repel a Bonapartist threat. Even the Bolsheviks for this purpose were acceptable allies, and they were allowed to form the Red Guard units which later became the main striking force in their seizure of power. This aid to the Provisional government rendered by the Bolsheviks enhanced their image as resolute defenders of the revolution and bolstered the SRs' and Mensheviks' naive belief that Lenin, after all, was one of them. In reality Lenin felt no loyalty to his brothers in revolution. Moreover, along with Kornilov's dismissal, the military leadership was drastically purged, leaving it with even less chance of repelling the later Bolshevik coup.

Before its re-emergence, the Bolshevik Party had already abandoned the slogan 'All Power to the Soviets', and resolved on preparations for an uprising. Some delegates to the Sixth Congress of the Party in August felt that Lenin was dangerously forcing the pace. Their misgivings were not allayed when in early autumn control of several important Soviets, including that of Moscow, passed to their party. The doubters saw in this evidence that the popularity of the Mensheviks and SRs was waning, but not that the people were yet ready for a one-party dictatorship. When the Bolshevik Central Committee resolved on 23 October that 'armed uprising is inevitable and the time is ripe' two members, Zinoviev and Kamenev, made public their disagreement. Others salved their consciences with the expectation that the new government would be a Bolshevik-led socialist coalition.

On the night of 7–8 November Red Guards and pro-Bolshevik troops, organized by Trotsky (who had thrown in his lot with his old rival in August), seized key points in the city. Kerensky, at the last moment, had announced plans for a Constituent Assembly and convened a preparatory 'pre-Parliament', but had refused to proclaim his intention of making an early peace or distributing land. When the Bolsheviks struck he fled, and his government was arrested in the Winter Palace. His reluctance, after the Kornilov affair, to bring in loyal troops while there was still time, or yet to woo the masses with promises of reform, delivered Russia into the hands of a tiny party whose main assets were fanatical leadership, nimble demagogy and tight internal discipline.

The uprising was timed for the eve of the Second All-Russian Congress of Soviets. As it turned out, the Bolsheviks and their potential allies held 380 out of 650 seats in that body: and when on 8 November the Mensheviks and right-wing SRs walked out in protest against the coup they were left unopposed. The Congress appointed a new government, the 'Council of People's Commissars', with Lenin as chairman, and voted for peace without annexations and indemnities, and for immediate land reform. These first Leninist decrees gave immense political strength to what was at first a mere military dictatorship, resting on the Red Guards and pro-Bolshevik soldiers. When the commander-in-chief refused to open negotiations with the Germans he was lynched by his troops and replaced by a Bolshevik junior officer. The Germans, hard pressed in the West, granted a preliminary armistice at Brest-Litovsk on 15 December. The decree on land abolished private ownership and authorized distribution of all private and church lands to the peasants by local committees. The terms of the decree, quite incompatible with traditional Marxist or earlier Leninist agrarian policy, were based on the demands of a Congress of Peasant Soviets held in May, and dominated by the SRs. In both decrees, Lenin was merely recognizing facts, and turning them to his advantage: the demoralized army was incapable of resisting a fresh German offensive, and the peasants had begun expropriation of the gentry months before. Together, the two decrees accelerated the disintegration of the armies at the front even before demobilization was ordered in December, and so temporarily disarmed generals who might contemplate a *coup de main*. Moreover, the decree on land enabled Lenin to broaden his government by bringing in commissars from the splinter-party of 'Left SRs', who were promised that they would not be overruled on agrarian matters.

By the end of the year the new government had extended its power, after fierce fighting in places, to most Russian urban centres, though the non-Russian periphery for the most part remained outside the control of Petrograd. The Bolsheviks relied on increasing support amongst the industrial workers, whose spontaneous take-over of factories was not discouraged, and amongst soldiers grateful to be employed in crushing the bourgeoisie at home rather than in fighting at the front. There was as yet little organized support in the countryside, but Lenin the land-giver could at least discount organized opposition amongst the peasantry. In December, as a precaution against possible challengers, the government armed itself with a 'shining sword': the Extraordinary Commission for Combating Counter-Revolution (Cheka), headed by an aristocratic Bolshevik, the Pole Felix Dzierzynski. After an interval of nine months Russia once again had a political police with powers of summary arrest, but with a quite unprecedented appetite for summary executions.

The elections to the Constituent Assembly in November gave over half the seats to right-wing Socialist Revolutionaries, while the Bolsheviks and the left SRs won fewer than a third. Lenin could however point to Bolshevik majorities in many urban areas, and also claimed that the pace of political change after November made the Assembly unrepresentative before it met on 18 January 1918. In his view it had no legitimate business except to hail the power of the Soviets and depart. Its opening session was suspended at 5 am by a guard commander who complained that his men were tired, and troops fired on a crowd protesting later in the day against the refusal to allow the Assembly to reconvene. The first and last semblance of a democratically elected parliament in Russia's history was given no chance to pronounce on Bolshevik policies, except for some cautious criticism of the peace talks at Brest-Litovsk.

Peace with Germany was Lenin's most urgent need, and he was willing to pay a heavy price for it, speculating in his wildly optimistic way that the strains of war would soon provoke revolution in Germany and that the final settlement would be between fraternal governments. Many of his colleagues were still more euphoric: a leftist faction was for carrying the Revolution westward by war (for which the Soviet regime had as yet neither men nor arms), while Trotsky's group favoured 'neither peace nor war', which might have done very well if the Germans had been ready to play this game. Only an admonitory German attack enabled Lenin to carry his resolution in the Central Committee, by one vote. Under the terms of the Brest-Litovsk Treaty the Soviet government renounced broad territories which it in fact did not control, including Finland, Poland, the Baltic States, Bessarabia, parts of Belorussia and the Ukraine. For safety's sake the government moved to Moscow. The left SRs resigned from the government in protest against the humiliating peace. In the summer of 1918 SR terrorists murdered the German ambassador and two senior Bolsheviks, and wounded Lenin himself. The 'Red Terror' which followed numbered the deposed Tsar and his family, held prisoners at Ekaterinburg, amongst its victims.

The 'breathing space' so dearly bought was of short duration. By August White generals were mustering armies in the borderlands and in Siberia, and the Allied Powers were making the first of their landings, intended originally to prevent German seizure of arms deposits and bases in Russia, and if possible to reconstitute an Eastern front. The sudden collapse of the Central Powers in November fanned Bolshevik fears that the victorious Allies would now mount an international crusade to overturn the first proletarian government. With these fears went equally unreal hopes that revolution in areas evacuated by the Germans, in the unstable new Polish Republic, and above all in disorganized Germany and the crumbling Hapsburg Empire, would throw up workers' governments, rescue the Soviet state from isolation, and help it to solve its nightmarish economic problems. Civil war raged in Russia for nearly three years. At times the Soviet regime seemed close to extinction and Lenin later said that its survival was a miracle. At one critical moment (in October 1919) simultaneous offensives from Estonia and the Southern steppes brought White armies to the neighbourhood of Petrograd and within striking distance of Moscow. In the summer of 1920, while the Red Army was engaged in the West against a revanchiste Poland bent on restoring its frontiers of 1772, the ablest of the White generals launched an offensive from the Southern steppes which Lenin described as 'enormously dangerous'.

The Civil War inflicted incalculable human and material losses on a country already shattered by the war with Germany. The Red Army alone lost 1 million men, with total mortality as a result of military action, famine and epidemics put at 8 million. At this cost the Bolsheviks preserved their power, and by the spring of 1921 had reassembled most of the old Russian Empire, except for the newly independent countries, Poland, Finland and the Baltic States; Bessarabia, restored to Roumania by the Allies; parts of Belorussia and the Ukraine which the Soviet government ceded to Poland under the Treaty of Riga (March 1921); and a strip of the Far Eastern littoral, from which the Japanese reluctantly withdrew under American pressure in 1922.

The Bolsheviks owed their survival partly to the incoherence of their enemies. The anti-Bolshevik political groups could never agree on a schedule of reforms which might attract mass support. The White armies around the periphery never achieved strategic co-ordination and had no industrial base. Political divisions at home, and the unpopularity of fresh military enterprises after 1918, as well as widespread working-class sympathy with the 'first workers' state', limited the support which Western governments could give to the White armies. None of the interventionist forces fought a major battle on Russian territory. Nevertheless, the Soviet government's triumph was above all due to Bolshevik organizing capacity. The Red Army, Trotsky's creation, enrolled 5 million men in 1918–19. Inadequately armed (its effective striking force was never more than 1 million) and trained and led into battle largely by former Tsarist officers watched over by Bolshevik political commissars, it none the less proved superior to the loosely disciplined and only fitfully enthusiastic White troops. The compact area under continuous Bolshevik control was converted into an armed camp, the nationalized industry, in so far as shortages of fuel and raw materials permitted it to function, was tightly geared to military needs. The peasant's produce was ruthlessly requisitioned at derisory prices, yet peasant unrest was held firmly in check. Food rationing, with differential norms determined by the usefulness of particular groups to the regime, was perhaps the most effective device for mobilizing and controlling the population. And the Cheka was tirelessly active in stamping out disaffection.

The Bolshevik coup bore little resemblance to any Marxist model of proletarian revolution. The old regime had shrivelled and fallen before the nation had reached political maturity.

Nothing could take its place and bring order into the chaos of war-wrecked Russia except a more efficient autocracy. The Party based 'proletarian power' on what it regarded as the petty-bourgeois illusions and on the political indifference of the peasant mass. The economic and political prerequisites for socialism, as Marxists had always understood them, were lacking. Lenin, in a moment of polemical bravado, could speak of having the revolution first and creating its prerequisites afterwards. The most convincing justification for the Bolshevik seizure of power is that the situation demanded the energetic and resolute leadership which only the Bolsheviks proved capable of giving: 'power was lying around in the streets and we picked it up'. Lenin's ideological conscience demanded other excuses. He argued that the people would rapidly come to accept socialist ideals and make great sacrifices for them. As the Civil War ended it seemed rather that the Bolsheviks were in danger of losing credit with an exhausted nation, that the sacrifices demanded were becoming unbearable. Peasant risings broke out in the province of Tambov and elsewhere in the autumn of 1920. Troops clashed with hungry workers in Petrograd early in 1921. Worst of all, mutineers at the naval base of Kronstadt, a former Bolshevik stronghold, on 28 February 1921 set up a Provisional Revolutionary Committee and called for the election of 'Soviets without Bolsheviks'. These warning signals, and the desperate economic plight of the country, made necessary the abandonment of 'war communism' for a 'tactical retreat' which included ideologically unpalatable concessions to the peasantry. Only a rigidly disciplined Party, sternly checking democratic stirrings even within its own ranks, could carry on the involved manoeuvres which would lead in the end to socialism.

Lenin's other excuse derived from the internationalist traditions of Marxism. The Russian revolution must be seen in an international perspective. The imperialist system had snapped in its weakest link. Other revolutions would follow in a chain reaction. The proletariat of advanced countries would join hands with their Soviet brothers and rescue the Bolsheviks from their dilemma: that of a Party with the most enlightened and progressive of policies ruling over the most ignorant and the poorest of large European countries. It was to ignite such revolutions that the Third (Communist) International was set up in March 1919.

9

The Third International

In the programmatic theses which he presented to a Bolshevik conference in April 1917 Lenin spoke of immediate steps towards the founding of the Third International:

It is the task of our Party, operating in a country where the Revolution has begun earlier than in other lands, to seize the initiative in founding the Third International which will finally break with the Defensists, and also wage a decisive struggle against the vacillating policies of the 'Centre'.

The first practical steps were the formation of a revolutionary federation of former prisoners of war in Russia, and shortly after the October Revolution the establishment of the section of International Revolutionary Propaganda, headed by the Canadian Reinstein. In 1918 left-wing socialists broke away to set up revolutionary communist parties in Finland, Hungary, Austria, Poland, Holland and Germany. The Bolsheviks watched the rising revolutionary wave with feverish expectancy. The political and economic chaos created by the collapse of the central powers, and to a lesser extent the mutinous mood of sections of the working class in France and Britain, fired their hopes that their own coup would find emulators elsewhere. What is more, they had no certainty of survival unless they succeeded in internationalizing the revolution. Lenin informed a Party congress in March 1918 that 'there would be no hope for the final victory of our revolution if it were to remain isolated, if there were no revolutionary movement in other countries'. The Bolsheviks could do little to aid revolutionaries elsewhere: for three years they were contained first by the continuing threat from Germany (in spite of the punitive Peace of Brest Litovsk, concluded in March 1918) and then by civil war.

It was only in January 1919 that the Bolsheviks issued invitations to an 'International Congress of Revolutionary Proletarian Parties'. Their decision to do so was precipitated by fears that the

Versailles powers would combine to crush them, and by the initiative of the British Labour Party in calling a conference of all member parties of the Second International to be held in Berne in February. The fifty-one delegates from thirty countries who gathered in Moscow on 2 March can hardly be called widely representative. According to Angelica Balabanoff, newly arrived from Italy:

> Among the so-called representatives [of countries other than Russia] only one – Eberlein – could be considered a genuine delegate. All the others had been designated by the Central Committee of the Russian Communist Party, and chosen from persons of different national origins: prisoners-of-war who had gone over to the Soviet camp, ex-émigrés who had returned to Russia years ago and lost all contact with their countries of adoption, adventurers of all kinds.

Eberlein in fact opposed the establishment of a new International at that stage, and Balabanoff expressed misgivings. But the majority eagerly accepted Lenin's assurance that the revolutionary tide was rising throughout Europe – witness not only the workers' council movement in Germany, but as further proof that Soviet governments were at hand in the oldest countries of capitalism – the British government's recognition of the Birmingham Council of Workers' Representatives as an economic organization! The congress declared that workers everywhere should break finally with the discredited opportunist parties, currently planning to unite their efforts in support of Wilsonian schemes against Soviet Russia, should set up communist parties and join in revolutionary struggle for the establishment of proletarian dictatorship, of which the Soviet state provided a universally valid model.

A document attached to the letter of invitation disseminated in January mainly inside Soviet Russia stated clearly what was to be the main difference between the Third International and its predecessors:

'The Congress must set up a centre of the Communist International [Comintern] which subordinates the interests of the movement in each country to the common interests of the Revolution on an international scale'. Lenin was determined to achieve from the outset that disciplined unity under a single central control for which Marx had striven in vain, and which the Second International by its very nature could never contemplate. The International was to be in effect a single worldwide Party, constructed on the model of the Bolshevik Party. This concept was elaborated in the famous '21 points' defining the conditions of admission, promulgated by the Second Congress in August 1920. Each member party was required to signalize its break with the old social democrats, and its acceptance of international leadership, by calling itself 'Communist Party of ———— (Section of the Third International)'. Each party must amongst other things organize itself according to the (Bolshevik) principles of democratic centralism, set up parallel with its overt structure an 'underground apparatus', periodically purge itself of petty bourgeois elements, endeavour to replace reformists and centrists with communists in all key post in the working-class movement, ensure that the whole activity of communists in parliament was subordinated to the 'interests of truly revolutionary propaganda and agitation'. Each party must adopt a programme embodying the policies of the International, which must be approved by the Executive Committee of the International, the final decision in case of dispute resting with Congress. All decisions of Congress or of the Executive Committee were binding on member parties, but the central organs must take account of the diverse conditions in which particular parties worked, and issue generally binding decisions 'only on questions where such decisions are possible'.

The drafters of this uncompromising document justified what they called 'iron, almost military discipline within parties, and the tight centralization of the whole movement, with the claim that 'in almost all countries of Europe and America the class struggle is entering the phase of civil war'. It was in fact only on Russian soil that civil war was raging in August 1920. It was only the Bolsheviks who were locked in struggle with the 'forces of capitalism', represented on this occasion by General Wrangel's White army, the Western intervention forces and Pilsudski's armies. Moreover, the Bolsheviks were nervous about the stability of their own regime as the strains of prolonged war began to show in sporadic revolts (the Kronstadt mutiny, the Antonov rising), and widespread passive resistance in the countryside. In Europe the post-war revolutionary upsurge was subsiding; but Lenin internationalized the wild hopes and fears of the Bolsheviks themselves. He said that the proletariat everywhere faced 'the last fight' for the triumph of communism: in reality, it was only Bolshevism which faced a fight (the last for some time) to ensure its survival. From the beginning, Comintern was Russocentric not only organizationally, but in its mentality. Even in the proceedings of the Second Congress we can discern that duality which was inherent in the Soviet situation and was to bedevil Comintern policy. Member parties were required to reshape themselves as instruments of revolution and adjust all their activities to revolutionary ends. At the same time, they were to bring pressure on governments to normalize relations with Soviet Russia. There was of course no theoretical incompatibility between the two requirements: Soviet Russia could serve as the advance post of world revolution only if it survived as a state among states. This dual role, however, was bound to create great difficulties both in Soviet relations with other countries, and in Comintern's relations with individual communist parties.

The subordination of local interests to those of the movement as a whole meant in effect subordination to the interests of the 'first workers' state'. It was left to Stalin to dismiss as obsolete Marx's dictum that 'the working man has no fatherland' and claim that 'the Soviet Union is the fatherland of the world's workers'; but as so often he was merely expressing Lenin's view more bluntly. Inevitably, it became the duty of foreign communists to adapt their actions to changing Soviet policies, which were always greatly affected by domestic exigencies and considerations. Thus, the first revolutionary phase of Comintern was over when the civil war and 'War Communism' ended in Russia. From 1921 to 1928 Comintern's 'united front' policy – complicated by sporadic revolutionary outbursts which Comintern did little to promote – was the international corollary of the New Economic Policy in Soviet Russia. The abrupt switch in 1929 to a new line of all-out revolutionary struggle was dictated less by any new development in international affairs than by the collectivization crisis in the Soviet Union. The Popular Front tactics adopted in 1935 were a belated reaction to the Nazi danger which the previous phase of Comintern policy had helped to create. In 1939 member parties of Comintern were required after the conclusion of the Ribbentrop–Molotov pact to refrain from provoking Germany and hamper the war effort of Western governments, until the German attack on the USSR converted the 'imperialist war' overnight into a struggle of democracy against fascism.

The headquarters of Comintern, for obvious reasons, could be nowhere except in Soviet Russia. All seven congresses were held in that country, and Moscow was the seat of the Executive Com-

1 *left* Karl Marx

2 & 3 Lenin's promise of peace was redeemed briefly at Brest-Litovsk, March, 1918. *above* Yoffe, Kamenev, Karakhan arriving. Soon, the White challenge, Ukrainian separatism, Polish territorial claims provoke mobilization of Red Army – Moscow 1918 *below*

4 At II Congress – Sylvia Pankhurst, John Reed (standing second from right

5 Bukharin at the funeral of John Reed, author of *Ten Days that shook the World* (died 1920)

6 The cult begins – Brodsky at work at III Congress of Comintern

mittee. The permanent apparatus, which included regional as well
as functional departments, was staffed largely by Russians and by
expatriates from countries where communism had been suppressed (Kuusinen, Dimitrov, Rakosi and Togliatti are examples),
some of whom became Soviet citizens. The Executive Committee
corresponded with parties abroad through diplomatic channels,
periodically sent emissaries to inspect and instruct them, maintained permanent representatives in some countries, and regularly
summoned foreign leaders for consultation. The pressures of
Comintern from the first bore heavily on foreign parties. The
Twenty-One Points drove some early member parties out of the
organization, and split others. Successive changes of line produced
schisms, expulsions of dissidents, demonstrative resignations. In
the twenties the lives of communist parties were complicated by
the commitment of their leaders to this or that faction in the
Soviet Communist Party. In most communist parties in the
twenties changes of leadership were frequent, and with the
enormous turnover of membership gradually shaped parties
which might or might not be effectual, but were certainly
obedient. True to the dictum which Lenin borrowed from Lassalle
that a party strengthens itself by purging itself, Comintern was
more interested in discipline than in size. Only in Germany did
the communists emerge as major contenders for political power,
and their chances were ruined by Comintern's misdirection. Elsewhere in Europe, the fortunes of Communism were boosted for a
while by the Popular Front, then again after another slump by the
Soviet Union's tremendous contribution to the defeat of Hitler,
and, more decisively, by the emergence of the Soviet Union as a
major power after the Second World War. Outside Europe, there
was only one firmly entrenched communist party – the Chinese,
after 1935 remote from Comintern and Soviet interference, idiosyncratic, destined to win power by its own efforts, and to shatter
irreparably the Russocentric concept of international communism.

Communists have no copyright in the word opportunism.
Lenin, in the most ordinary sense, was a supreme opportunist, a
virtuoso of manoeuvre and manipulation, ready for an immediate
political advantage to form the most unlikely and insincere
alliances, to adopt for a while policies which contradicted his
firmest convictions. One such alliance (with the left SR party) and
one such policy (general distribution of land to the peasants) kept
him in power after the coup of October 1917. The first proletarian

c

and socialist revolution was precariously based on the peasants' proprietorial ambitions. Excuses for Lenin (as well as arguments against him) can always be found in Marx. At one stage, Marx had encouraged the idea that a peasant revolution might result in the establishment of socialism in Russia if it were quickly followed by proletarian revolutions in more advanced countries. Lenin of course did not invoke this pronouncement, or call his revolution 'agrarian', but he looked as we know for revolution elsewhere, and especially in Germany, to ensure his success. Again, Marx had put forward a sketchy but highly suggestive theory of 'permanent revolution', and in 1917 Lenin had his own derivative version: the peasant mass, rapidly disillusioned with smallholding, would come over to the proletariat and fight with it for socialism and against the rural bourgeoisie. The supporting revolutions did not happen, and no significant section of the peasantry was converted to socialism. And so, in 1921, Lenin, for irresistibly powerful economic and social reasons, found it necessary to win the peasantry all over again with fresh concessions: trade was freed (taxation replaced arbitrary requisitioning), the leasing of land and hiring of labour was permitted. This tactical retreat seemed to many communists a betrayal, and to hopeful anti-communists a statesmanlike acknowledgement of defeat. Lenin soon produced another rationalization: all-embracing and interdependent consumer and producer co-operatives, the spread of education and the example of properous state farms would painlessly convert the peasant into a socialist. The results of the 'great co-operative plan' were negligible, the peasant remained obstinately petty bourgeois, and in 1929 Stalin seized control of agriculture by what he himself called a 'second revolution', a 'revolution from above', 'no less important than the October Revolution'. The Bolsheviks enjoy no exemption from the rule that ends are conditioned by, and often are a mere continuation of, the means used to achieve them. For the Social Democrats, peaceful political struggle, for the Bolsheviks dictatorial social engineering, became not means but ends in themselves.

Leninist opportunism characterized Bolshevik policy abroad as much as at home. The path to world socialism must twist and turn, detours and setbacks and retreats were to be expected. The situation was much more complex than that which Marx and Engels had contemplated. Other Marxists, besides Bernstein, recognized that capitalism had undergone profound changes since the death of Marx. The phenomenon which Rosa Luxemburg, Kautsky and Lenin all considered most significant was that of 'Imperialism'. Lenin's analysis of the 'highest stage of capitalism' provided him with a refutation of Bernstein, a justification for socialist revolution in a backward country, and a complex strategy for world revolution. Marx and Engels could blithely regard the economic and political development of two or three advanced countries as decisive for socialism everywhere. Lenin found assurance of ultimate victory 'on the world scale' in the interaction between three sets of 'capitalist contradictions': those between capitalist and proletariat in each country, those between capitalist countries, and those between capitalist countries and colonial or semi-colonial areas. It was the exploitation of backward countries that had given capitalism a stay of execution, smoothed out the curve of economic crisis, and since the capitalists had used some of their loot to bribe their own workers into quiescence, had created a breeding ground for opportunism. But this new prosperity was specious and transistory. There were no more 'blank spots on the map', and capitalist greed must lead to wars for the redivision of colonies and markets, which would revolutionize the temporarily dormant proletariat, especially in defeated countries. Moreover, the national independence movements in backward countries would help to undermine the economic position of the exploiting powers, and swell the ranks of the revolutionary anti-capitalist alliance. The first workers' state must exploit all three sets of capitalist contradictions, but it must proceed cautiously, since the capitalists would be tempted to sink their differences in a common anti-Soviet crusade. Lenin insisted that a series of frightful clashes would precede the final triumph of communism, and that in the meantime the Soviet state must co-exist with more or less hostile powers, trade wherever the best terms were offered, even if necessary ally itself with politically incompatible countries to split a potential anti-Soviet bloc, above all avoid isolation. Obviously, good relations with a bourgeois government, whether in an advanced capitalist country or a backward country struggling for independence, might demand sacrifices from the local communist party. But for Lenin in his last years, and for his successors, there was no contradiction between the two roles of the soviet state: its survival and growth above all guaranteed the final triumph of the world revolutionary movement. Comintern renounced the particularist opportunism of the old social democrats, but its revolutionary internationalism merely cloaked Soviet opportunism. As a result, after brief periods when it achieved a semblance of disciplined unity, international communism would again fragment, local interests opportunistically pursued would triumph over pseudo-internationalism, and once again world revolution would prove to be an infinitely receding mirage.

part 2
The Revolutionary Phase

1

Germany

For the Bolsheviks in the years 1918–21 the political future of Germany was supremely important. The peace of Brest-Litovsk gave them breathing space – while greatly reducing their territory – but no guarantee that Imperial Germany would not turn again and destroy them. The victory of the Allied Powers removed this danger, but created another: that they would convert their limited and precautionary intervention in Russia into an anti-Bolshevik crusade. Revolution and the establishment of a proletarian dictatorship in Germany would transform the strategic position, neutralize or bring down the hostile regime in newly independent Poland, and give the Bolsheviks the support of a highly industrialized country in creating the economic base for socialism.

Superficially, the situation in Germany in the autumn of 1918 resembled that in Russia some eighteen months earlier. The Kaiser abdicated, the country was declared a republic, socialists formed a provisional government with the connivance of the generals, and Workers' and Soldiers' Councils sprang up everywhere. The Bolsheviks hoped that the right-wing leaders of the SPD, discredited by their commitment to the disastrous war, would be unable to satisfy or contain the turbulent and hungry masses, and would be swept away by the Councils. But the similarities between Germany and Russia were fortuitous and ephemeral, the differences deep-seated and decisive. In Russia, there had been no alternative framework of authority when the autocracy collapsed, no tradition of disciplined and coherent political activity. In Germany the SPD itself was one of the powerful factors for stability. The 'German revolution' ended almost as soon as it had begun. It was 'betrayed' by the SPD, according to communist historians and some latter-day German radicals preoccupied with the faults and failures of the Weimar Republic. But, in putting down sporadic extremist outbreaks and working for bourgeois democracy rather than proletarian dictatorship, the SPD was again correctly interpreting the mood of the masses, just as it had in voting for war credits in 1914. Its followers – and this meant the majority of workers – were content with the proclamation of the Republic, the promise of parliamentary democracy, the reassuring presence of Social Democrats at the centre of power. They had little appetite for further great upheavals, and for the most part no urge to wrest responsibility for their own well-being from the politicians. Most Workers' and Soldiers' Councils saw themselves as emergency organs of local government, followed the lead of the Social Democratic ministers, and looked to the future National Assembly to settle the new political order. The weakness of the extreme socialist left was clearly shown by the events of December 1918–January 1919.

The war had deepened the ideological cracks within the SPD, but the fetish of party unity delayed organizational cleavage. Even in 1914 a minority amongst the socialist deputies voted for war credits only reluctantly, and only to avoid a breach of party discipline. As the war continued the left-centrist group within the Party became more and more critical of the leadership, and from December 1915 refused to vote further military credits, but still could not bring itself to condemn the war outright. A smaller faction around Karl Liebknecht and Rosa Luxemburg was uncompromisingly hostile to the collaborationist leadership, and from April 1915 condemned Social Democratic connivance at the war as a crime against the proletariat of all lands. The imprisonment of the group's leaders did not put an end to their agitation. Indeed, the name by which they were best known – Spartakists – was taken from Rosa Luxemburg's 'Spartakus letters' written in gaol and circulated in the autumn of 1916. But these extremists, as well as the centrists, sought a formula which would enable them both to retain freedom of expression and to remain in the parent organization. A formal split came only when the SPD leadership, on the insistence of the Supreme Command, tried to restore discipline and silence its critics. The Party Council ruled that, by holding an unauthorized conference at Gotha in April 1917, the two groups had put themselves outside the SPD. It was only then that the dissidents nerved themselves to form a new Independent Socialist Party (USPD).

This uneasy alliance of centrists and Spartakists was upset by the 'revolutionary' events of November–December 1918. On 18 November the Spartakist newspaper *Rote Fahne* published Rosa

Luxemburg's article 'The Beginning', in which she called for the transference of all power to the Workers' and Soldiers' Councils and the continuation of revolutionary struggle – 'thumb upon the eye and knee upon the chest' – for the abolition of capitalism and the establishment of a socialist order. But on 19 December the National Congress of Workers' and Soldiers' Councils decided, by 400 votes to 50, in favour of elections to a Constituent Assembly. Rosa Luxemburg's reaction was to vilify the Congress as 'Mamelukes of Ebert' (the Social Democratic Minister President), and to discern evidence of growing revolutionary ferment in the street-fighting, hooliganism and looting prevalent in Berlin and other large centres of population. Her hopes of radicalizing the USPD at large were dashed when on 24 December its leaders rejected her demand for a special congress to discuss the Party's campaign for the election to the National Assembly. The Spartakists resolved to break with the USPD, and to merge with another extremist group, the Left Radicals based on Bremen, and under the ideological tutelage of Karl Radek, who, like Rosa Luxemburg, had played a part in the Polish, German and Russian socialist movements, but unlike her was an unqualified admirer and supporter of Lenin. At a joint conference held between 29 December 1918 and 1 January 1919 the Spartakists and Left Radicals established the Communist Party of Germany (KPD).

Rosa Luxemburg and Leo Jogiches, her intimate collaborator for nearly three decades, both doubted the timeliness of this move. She had always disliked the Leninist concept of the elite party, insisted that revolutionaries must accurately interpret the mood of the masses, soldiered on in the increasingly uncongenial SPD for fear of disrupting socialist unity and losing contact with the rank and file. Now she was the leader of a splinter group of revolutionary intellectuals, whose popular support numbered a few thousands. Its leader – and its prisoner, for the majority at the Foundation Congress rejected her recommendation that the newborn KPD should take part in the elections to the National Assembly. Her reasoning, close to that which Lenin had used to justify Bolshevik participation in the Duma, was that 'the elections and the floor of the Assembly must be used to mobilize the masses against the Assembly'. Here she was true to her lifelong principle of seeking the closest contact with the masses and trying to lead them by persuasion. But her hot-headed followers put her in a paradoxical position. Democratic loyalty to the majority

65

decision of a tiny group (the KPD attracted fewer than 100,000 members in the first two years of its existence) committed her to persist in calling for the transference of power to the Councils, in which a majority representing many millions of workers had democratically refused to supplant the National Assembly. Not surprisingly, she looked eagerly for signs that the masses were in fact more revolutionary than their leaders.

In January 1919 the dismissal of the Berlin police chief (a member of the USPD) provoked demonstrations and disorders in the city, in which anarchists, bandits and hooligans were quite as active as organized workers. The KPD, together with some independent socialists and the Revolutionary Shop Stewards, issued a call for the overthrow of the government. The Social Democrat Noske, People's Commissar responsible for military affairs, called in troops who quickly quelled the riots. 'Order rules in Berlin', wrote Rosa Luxemburg in *Rote Fahne* on 14 January. 'Stupid lackeys! Your order is built on sand! Tomorrow the revolution will rise again and proclaim with brazen trumpets: I was, I am, I shall be!' On the following day Karl Liebknecht and Rosa Luxemburg were arrested in their hiding place and on the way to the Moabit prison savagely ill-treated and murdered. A highly respectable German newspaper saw this as a fitting end for 'criminals pure and simple who ... had long lost all ability to distinguish between good and evil'. There was, however, widespread revulsion against the crime, even among political enemies of the murdered leaders. But only two of the soldiers responsible were indicted, and only on minor charges.

Rosa Luxemburg's oldest and closest collaborator, Leo Jogiches, was shot dead in March 1919 while under interrogation in a police station, and leadership of the infant party passed to the young lawyer Paul Levi. His brilliance as a polemical writer and speaker, his keen intelligence and his firmness won him to begin with the respect of Lenin and the Bolsheviks. He succeeded in reversing the Party's earlier decisions on non-participation in parliamentary and trade union activity, though not without a split: a diehard leftist faction broke away to become the 'Communist Workers' Party' (KAPD). To the annoyance of Levi and his successors, this small splinter group was cautiously tolerated by Comintern, and even at times played off against the orthodox Party.

The infant KPD in its first two years was puny and ineffectual. It held back when in March 1920 a general strike was called to defeat the rightwing Kapp *putsch*. *Rote Fahne's* rhetoric on this occasion would find echoes in a more fearful crisis a decade later. The proletariat should 'not lift a finger' to save the democratic republic which was a 'cracked mask for capitalist dictatorship'. In fact, the proletariat gave overwhelming support to the trade unions, and the KPD changed its mind – too late to win any credit. The weakness of the Party was clearly demonstrated in June, when in the first Reichstag elections it gained 2 seats, as compared with the 102 of the SPD, and the 84 of the USPD. Later in the year, however, the Party's fortunes improved dramatically. After preliminary discussions in Moscow the USPD held a congress at Halle in October, which decided (by 236 votes to 156) to join Comintern. The rank and file of the Party proved to be less powerfully attracted by Comintern than their Congress representatives: only 300,000 (rather more than a third) followed the left-wing leaders into the KPD in December. None the less, the KPD, swollen overnight from 50,000 to 350,000 members, had at last some claim to be considered a mass party.

Levi, however, still believed that the Party must work patiently to develop its strength before taking political risks. He did not share the view, common to the left wing of his Party and some of the Comintern leaders, that revolution was just around the corner.

In January 1921, in the famous Open Letter which anticipated Comintern's later 'united front' tactics, he (vainly) urged other working-class organizations to concert with the KPD a schedule of demands upon the government. He organized spectacular and highly emotional demonstrations on the anniversary of the deaths of Luxemburg and Liebknecht. He, like Lenin, had condemned 'National Bolshevism' – the idea of a military alliance between bourgeois Germany and Soviet Russia against the Versailles powers, which had its supporters both on the left and on the right in Germany. But he himself called for the solidarity of 'oppressed nations' (including Germany) against the oppressors, and played on German resentment of Versailles. He was intent on building up an image of the KPD as a party of responsible militancy in the interests of the masses and the nation. His political career was however cut short in the early months of 1921.

In January Levi attended and played an important part in the Congress of the Italian Socialist Party at Leghorn. The PSI had adhered to Comintern in 1919, and was now required in accordance with the 'twenty-one conditions of membership' adopted in

June 1920, to purge itself of its large right wing. The leader of the majority, Serrati, feared that too sudden a break would alienate too large a section of the Party: and Levi supported him against the bullying Comintern envoys Rakosi (Hungarian) and Kabakchiev (Bulgarian). As Levi had foreseen, Comintern's high-handedness converted one of its strongest member parties (in terms of electoral support) into a politically insignificant, and still ideologically unstable, rump. Radek, who turned up in Berlin to rebuke Levi on his return, admitted that it was now a 'mistake to suppose that we have an Italian communist party'. This did not, of course, prevent Radek, and the Central Committee of the KPD (by a narrow majority), from condemning Levi's breach of discipline. Levi promptly resigned, together with four other of the fourteen members of the *Zentrale* (the executive directorate of the Central Committee).

Radek on this occasion repeated the vague hint he had made in the manifesto drafted for the Unification Congress that the KPD should be 'activated'. A leftist faction around Ruth Fischer, Arkadi Maslow and Ernst Reuter had found Levi's realism irksome. The Party had begun organizing clandestine sections as required by the 'twenty-one conditions', and they too were eager for action.

The impatience of the Party was also no doubt increased by the influx of left USPD members, who unlike the Spartakists had not experienced the sobering disaster of January 1919. In the early months of 1921 galloping inflation, rising unemployment, the inability of the central government to suppress right wing 'home guard' units in Bavaria, and popular resentment caused by the punitive French occupation of three Ruhr towns and the approaching plebiscite in Upper Silesia, convinced the hotheads in the KPD that a revolutionary situation was fast maturing. This was an illusion which some of the Comintern and Soviet leaders were eager to share. Radek, in Berlin in January, explained Comintern's demand for 'activation' by concern that the revolution should come before Germany was economically ruined and the masses doomed to prolonged poverty: but the real reason was probably one at which he hinted – anxiety about the security of the Soviet regime itself in face of growing unrest amongst the workers and peasants. However this may be, in March three Comintern envoys – the Hungarians, Kun and Pogany, and the Pole, Góralski (Kleine) – arrived in Berlin to energize the German leadership. The three 'Turkestaner', as some German communists irreverently called them, were chosen not for their understanding of the German situation, which was negligible, nor presumably for their revolutionary record, which contained nothing but dismal failures, but for their total dependence on Moscow.

These adventurers by proxy, and the new *Zentrale* which combined a yearning for action with a quite remarkable organizational incapacity, were responsible for the fiasco known as 'the March action'. The first blow, however, was struck by the Prussian government, which in association with the local civil administration ordered a police occupation of Prussian Saxony. The traditional militancy of this major industrial area had been aggravated by a massive immigration of unemployed workers from Western Germany. In Halle, and some other towns, the communists were the strongest working-class party, and turbulent leftists dominated the local organizations. The *Zentrale* not only supported their call for strikes in protest against the police occupation but worked to convert these demonstrations into an insurrection. Hugo Eberlein ('Hugo with the Fuse') was dispatched from Berlin to dynamite buildings, railway lines, or trains carrying explosives, and inflame public feeling against the police, who would, it was thought, be automatically blamed for these outrages. The local Party organizations, however, proved ineffectual both as dynamiters and as strike leaders. The occupation and fortification of the great Leuna works at Merseburg, which led to the declaration of a state of emergency, was the only major communist success. More effectively disruptive and destructive were the armed bands, mainly of rootless unemployed, rallied by the freelance revolutionary Max Hoelz, who had been expelled from the KPD earlier and now had closer relations with the KAPD. Outside Saxony, there were serious disturbances in Hamburg and in the Rhineland. The Hamburg events were perhaps even more worrying for the KPD than for the government, since the seizure of the shipyards led to clashes between unemployed and employed workers. Elsewhere, the *Zentrale*'s call for a nationwide general strike met with a poor response. By the end of the month the 'action' had petered out. The reprisals which followed fell much more heavily on the rank and file than on the KPD leaders. As the government perhaps intended, revulsion against the leaders caused a mass exodus from the Party, which in a matter of months was reduced to a membership of 180,443.

The 'March action' was bitterly criticized by Levi's supporters, the most influential of whom, Klara Zetkin, demanded an end to 'revolutionary calisthenics'. They failed, however, to carry a vote of censure in the Central Committee. Levi himself, in a caustic pamphlet called 'Our Path', described the action as 'the biggest Bakuninist putsch in history', was expelled from the KPD for again failing to disguise his superior common sense, and spent the rest of his political career as a left wing Social Democrat.

The findings at Comintern's inquest were that Hermann Brandler and his colleagues had quite rightly reacted to government aggression, but had not handled the situation very skilfully. The responsibility of Comintern itself, and particularly of its emissaries in Berlin, was glossed over.

A leftist group in the KPD had represented the March action as an application of what they called the 'theory of the offensive'. By this they meant that only by taking the offensive could the Party discover and mobilize its potential mass support. This notion, condemned by Comintern, neatly sums up the dilemma of the KPD. The Party could not compete with the SPD in the normal peaceful functions of working-class organization: the day-to-day struggle for better wages and working conditions, the provision of welfare services and social facilities, representation of working class interests in relations with government and employers. The KPD existed to carry out a revolution, and all its short-term activities were ancillary to this purpose, not an end in themselves. As a result, the Party was shunned by the mass of the workers. Yet the Party could grow only by weaning away support from non-revolutionary socialists and trade unionists. In order to do so, it must show itself a more ardent champion of immediate working-class interests. This would involve tactical co-operation with other socialist organizations, but always with the ultimate aim of exposing their leaders as instruments of the exploiters, and of converting the masses to revolution as the only means of radically improving their lot. While co-operating with reformist socialists in order eventually to discredit them and capture their followers, the Party must not neglect its preparations for revolution, and in particular must build up a paramilitary striking force.

In the 'united front' phase of Comintern strategy, the KPD was trapped between two dangers. Impatience for revolutionary action might find an outlet in disastrous adventures. On the other hand, excessive flexibility in the competitive co-operation with non-communists might result in the blurring of revolutionary ideology, complacent acceptance of limited objectives, indefinite postponement of major battles.

In 1921–3 a leftist faction around Ruth Fischer, Arkadi Maslow and Ernst Thälmann was openly sceptical about 'united front' tactics, and particularly about the idea of a coalition 'workers' government' entertained by Brandler and the dominant group in the *Zentrale*. In 1923, Brandler's concept was briefly realized in two German states, and simultaneously the KPD was hustled by Comintern into the third and last of its revolutionary adventures.

The crisis of 1923 in Germany was similar to that of 1921, but deeper and more damaging. To speed up payment of reparations, French armies occupied the Rhineland. Inflation raged uncontrollably: workers were sometimes paid several times daily and carried away sacks of paper which depreciated further before they reached home. Unemployment figures soared, and in some areas food was dangerously short. The Cuno government called for passive resistance to the French, but was clearly incapable of reaching an international settlement. In return for the promise of a loan the government contemplated concessions to industrialists which would bear hard on the already desperate workers. The feeble democracy was threatened by right-wing agitators with paramilitary formations behind them, and openly encouraged by some of the old generals in Bavaria (where Hitler, backed by Ludendorff, was winning his first success), and in North Germany. A separatist movement gained strength in the Rhineland. At midsummer the collapse of the Weimar regime seemed imminent, and the break-up of the Reich, civil war, or much heavier foreign intervention were all possibilities.

The KPD in this situation showed great versatility. It assumed once again the accents of injured national pride, denouncing the Cuno government as a tool of the Entente as well as of German capitalism, and (on Radek's inspiration) hailing as a martyr a certain Schlageter, a Freikorps lieutenant utterly remote from the working class or the left, who was shot by the French. Through its control commissions in enterprises and its network of factory committees the Party tried to take the lead in strikes and demonstrations, and draw the social democratic workers after it. At the same time the Party, with the help of dozens of Russian advisers including General Skoblevsky, built up an elaborate military

71

apparatus. Its main striking force would be the 'proletarian hundreds', which in the course of the year drew in some 100,000 members. The main political base of the Party's activities was Central Germany, where the left-wing socialist governments of Saxony and Thuringia relied on communist support in the Diet.

In August Cuno fell, and a strong coalition government, including Social Democrats, was formed under Stresemann. The government shortly decided to end passive resistance in the Ruhr and, to protect itself against extremists on the right and the left, on 26 September had the President declare a state of emergency. The Defence Minister, General Gessler, was entrusted with 'supreme executive power', and delegated overriding regional authority to the commanders of the seven military districts. Their most immediate task was to bring the regional police forces under central control and to draw the teeth of the left-wing and right-wing paramilitary formations. Gessler chose to begin with Red Saxony rather than Bavaria, where the state government, encouraged by the former regional Wehrmacht commanders, was defiant, and extremist nationalism was rapidly gaining strength. Communists, inevitably, saw Gessler's order of priorities as evidence of a partiality for fascism, but this explanation was shown to be absurd by the government's subsequent firm action in Bavaria. In September and October the government moved first against Central Germany because it was closer to hand, because the behaviour of the Saxon government might tempt the Bavarian wildmen to provoke a civil war, and because the KPD entrenched itself in Germany with openly proclaimed revolutionary intentions.

Brandler spent part and perhaps the whole of September in Moscow, where the combined efforts of his own left wing (Fischer, Maslow and Thälmann) and of the Comintern leadership convinced him, apparently against his better judgement, that the hour of revolution was at hand. On 1 October, Zinoviev telegraphed Comintern's instructions to the *Zentrale* in Berlin. The 'decisive moment', he said, was only 'four, five or six weeks' away. The communists must enter the Saxon and Thuringian governments if they were willing to defend Saxony against 'Bavaria and the Fascists' and must arm workers in preparation. Fatuous optimism, in situations where he ran no personal risk, was habitual to Zinoviev. But on this occasion the much shrewder Trotsky also exerted his powers of agitation on Brandler. Stalin, a third contender for the mantle of the stricken Lenin, was at first dubious, but in the general atmosphere of revolutionary excitement he wrote to Thalheimer a letter published on 10 October in *Rote Fahne*, speaking of the 'approaching revolution in Germany', which would 'have a greater importance for the proletariat of Europe and America than the Russian revolution six years ago', and would 'undoubtedly shift the centre of world revolution from Moscow to Berlin'.

The *Zentrale* moved from Berlin to Dresden, and communist ministers entered the socialist governments of Saxony (10 October) and Thuringia (13 October). In Saxony, Brandler himself took a post which gave him access to police files. Their plan was to steel their socialist colleagues in resistance to the central government's demands for the disbandment of the proletarian hundreds. At the critical moment a nationwide general strike would be called in protest against attempts to disarm the workers in face of rampant fascism. Clashes between the police, the Wehrmacht and the fascist bands on the one hand, and armed workers on the other, would light the fires of revolution throughout Germany.

This plan had three main weaknesses. Firstly, the socialist ministers in Saxony and Thuringia, though they indignantly resisted the 'unconstitutional' encroachments of the central government, had no appetite for armed defiance, and the socialist and trade union organizations would not act without lengthily sounding the opinion of their membership. Secondly, the proletarian hundreds, in point of numbers, weapons and training, were far too weak to take on the forces at the disposal of the central government, not to mention the illegal right-wing formations. Thirdly, and most important, the second Stresemann cabinet, formed on 6 October, again with socialist participation, inspired hopes of economic recovery, and of a fair deal for workers, strong enough at least to make revolutionary chaos an unattractive alternative.

On 20 October the Reichswehr began its occupation of Saxony to restore order. At a hastily convened conference of labour representatives Brandler's demand for an immediate general strike was rejected. The majority insisted on preliminary negotiations with working-class organizations. While these were in progress, the KPD in Hamburg, apparently acting on false reports that a general strike had in fact begun in Saxony, began an armed uprising in the early hours of 23 October. Though the combat squads succeeded in occupying most of the city's police stations, the population at large, including even the dockers who were on strike, remained passive, the rising degenerated into sporadic street battles on the outskirts, and finally petered out on 25 October.

In the meantime the *Zentrale* had fled from Dresden to Berlin. There a Comintern delegation headed by Radek held the ring in a furious debate between Ruth Fischer's group, who were for a mass strike in Berlin as the prelude to a general uprising, and the painfully sobered right, who were for a quick retreat. After three days of debate the *Zentrale* issued a resolution which admitted that the working class at large was not ready for the fight, yet declared that the decisive struggle might begin any day, called on communists to continue negotiations with Social Democrats to 'force them into battle' or else drive a wedge between the workers and the socialist leaders, and urged them to support 'spontaneous working class action', while avoiding armed combat where possible. Once again, the Party was fighting on paper a battle for which it had no forces in the field.

On 29 October the Reichspresident used his powers under the federal constitution to dismiss the Saxon government, which had remained both obdurate and inert. A protest strike called by communists and left-wing socialists collapsed in a day. Radek's call for massive demonstrations in Berlin was not supported by the now thoroughly disheartened *Zentrale*. Germany's 'Red October' had ended in utter rout for the KPD, and humiliation for the Comintern leadership which much more directly and openly than in 1921 had committed its most important Western party to misconceived and ludicrously ill-planned revolutionary action.

With this débâcle the heroic age of German communism was over. The Stresemann government's resolute action against Rhenish separatists and against nationalists and fascists in Bavaria, its success in stabilizing the currency, raising foreign loans, and reaching a new *modus vivendi* with France, gave Germany a period of relative equilibrium. The KPD found itself more and more circumscribed: 12·6 per cent of the electorate voted for it in the May 1924 elections to the Reichstag, but only 9 per cent in December 1924, and 6·3 per cent in the presidential election of April 1925. Disoriented by Stresemann's stabilization, and torn by factional squabbles, the KPD leadership gave no firm direction to the Party.

The quarrels within the KPD interacted with the power

struggle in the Soviet Union which began even before Lenin's death in January 1924. Zinoviev, with his usual agile unscrupulousness, had made Brandler and Radek his scapegoats in the inquest on the October débâcle, and even put some blame on Trotsky, who was less responsible than he. Brandler's fall had the paradoxical result of reinforcing the wild left in the KPD. Zinoviev, rather reluctantly, accepted Fischer and Maslow as the Party's chosen leaders, while secretly urging Thälmann, as a true proletarian, to keep a close watch on these unstable intellectuals. Fischer and Maslow strove to endear themselves to Moscow by energetically implementing the programme of Bolshevization decreed by Comintern at its Fifth Congress in July 1924, which involved reduction of inner party democracy in the interests of discipline, the building up of a departmentalized professional party bureaucracy, and the creation of party cells in industry tightly controlled from the centre. This campaign gave them an opportunity to eliminate or immobilize many old Spartakists, who were attached to their founder's, Rosa Luxemburg's, concept of party democracy, and – as she had been except for one fatal lapse – were averse to revolutionary adventures. Fischer did not hesitate to describe 'Luxemburgism' as a 'syphilitic bacillus in the communist movement', and attacked it simultaneously with 'Trotskyism'. The dominant left proved too cautious as well as too dictatorial for an ultra-left group, represented in the *Zentrale* by Sholem, Rosenberg and Katz. Both left and ultra-left were swept away in the tidal wave caused by Zinoviev's fall. An impressively hyprocritical 'Open Letter' from the Executive Committee of Comintern, published in *Rote Fahne* on 1 September 1925 without the prior knowledge of the KPD, condemned Fischer and her friends for driving the KPD into isolation and demolishing inner party democracy. They had by now made themselves widely unpopular, and the Party readily replaced them by a group in which their proletarian watchdog Thälmann was the strongest personality. In the next two years the left and the ultra-left were eliminated in the course of a struggle which, in Hanover in January 1926, degenerated into street fighting between supporters of Comintern and of Katz.

This upheaval was followed by the promotion of many moderate communists to leading positions, and in March 1927 the Party held a 'congress of concentration' to rally all its forces behind a coalition in which Thälmann and his group shared power with the 'centrists' Meyer and Ewert. The alliance was short lived. Early in 1928 Thälmann denounced his colleagues as would-be 'conciliators' of the right. Once again, events in the KPD mirrored those in Moscow. Stalin's struggle with Bukharin and the Soviet 'right' was developing, and the CPSU informed a KPD delegation that 'the right danger is the main danger in the German workers' movement'. Thälmann's opponents fought back, and found an ugly weapon to hand. Thälmann had tried to hush up his brother-in-law's embezzlement of Party funds in the Wasserkante district of Hamburg. In September 1928 the Central Committee of the KPD, with only one abstention, relieved him and some of his supporters of their functions. Stalin, however, intervened to save him, and insisted through Comintern on his reinstatement.

Thälmann could rely on the support of the professional Party bureaucracy who now dominated congresses of the KPD and whose livelihood depended on Moscow's favour. A proletarian, an anti-intellectual, and an imposing speaker, he could carry off the role of Führer for which Stalin had cast him more naturally than Stalin himself. As an ex-leftist he was exhilarated by the end of the 'united front' policy, decreed by Stalin, and the beginning of a 'class against class' struggle in which the Social Democrats, now termed 'social fascists', were the immediate enemy. The Party Congress of June 1929 was conducted on the Soviet model. Thälmann was greeted with a 'stormy ovation' the singing of the Internationale, and a triple 'Heil Moskau!' chanted by a youth delegation.

The new policy caused much confusion amongst the rank and file who frequently clashed with Nazi bands, and occasional difficulties between Comintern and the German leadership. None the less, Thälmann and his closest colleagues, Neumann and Remmele, hewed to the Moscow line. A resolution of the 'Political Bureau' (as the *Zentrale* was now called) published on 15 June 1930 declared that:

> Fascism in Germany is by no means limited to the combat and murder organizations of the National Socialists, the Stahlhelm, etc., but includes all important bourgeois parties. The fascization of Germany is being carried out not only through the combat organizations but also through the bourgeois state apparatus and its social-fascist [i.e. Social Democratic] agents.

The resolution further demanded that a distinction should be drawn between the Nazi leaders and their following, and condemned the slogan 'smite the fascists wherever you find them!' In April 1931 Stalin criticized the KPD in Thuringia for joining the Social Democrats in a vote of no confidence against Wilhelm Frick, the Nazi Minister of the Interior. When in the summer of 1931 the Nazis and certain right-wing groups organized a plebiscite to bring down the Social Democratic government in Prussia, the KPD on instructions from Moscow organized a 'red plebiscite' of its own to the same purpose. *Rote Fahne* on occasions noted with gratification examples of co-operation between Nazi and communist workers in the struggle against 'industrialists and the social democrat trade union bonzes', and the Party even addressed a friendly appeal to rank and file brownshirts, pictured as misled but honest patriots.

This disastrous policy is explained in part by a chronic underestimation of Nazism. Thälmann inferred from Hitler's temporary electoral setback in 1932 that he was doomed to defeat, and insisted more confidently than ever that social democracy was the important adversary. Even in the spring of 1933 Wilhelm Pieck said that 'if the Nazis come to power they will be at the end of their tether in two months, and it will be our turn', and Fritz Heckert, the German representative to Comintern, echoed this conviction. Stalin may have had a different opinion. Late in 1931 he enquired of Neumann whether he agreed that 'if the "Nationalists" seize power they will be so completely occupied with the West that we can build socialism here in peace?' But as a rule he encouraged the KPD leaders to believe that the crisis would polarize the masses in Germany, wreck the Social Democratic party and drive its supporters into the communist camp for future battles with fascism. They professed to find evidence for this belief in the rapid growth of the Party (membership rose from 124,511 in 1929 to 180,000 in 1931 and 332,000 in 1932) and its increasing electoral strength. But the Nazis won more votes than the communists in the Reichstag elections of 1929 (18·3 per cent as against 13·1 per cent), twice as many in November 1932 (33·1 per cent as against 16·8 per cent), and in March 1933 their electoral support (43·9 per cent) comfortably exceeded that of the social democrats (18·3 per cent) and the communists (12·3 per cent) together.

The exiled Trotsky, helplessly deploring the wilful and suicidal myopia of the KPD, said that earlier the social democrats had rejected a united front with the communists against fascism, and now the communists had in effect formed a united front with fascism against social democracy. Whether co-operation between communists and social democrats against Hitler would have been effective is an unanswerable question. What is certain is that by faithfully following Stalin's instructions, and making the socialists their main enemy, the communists gravely weakened the forces of resistance to fascism. They paid dearly for their mistake. After Hitler's victory the Party claimed that it had suffered no irreparable defeat, but had tactically retired underground. In fact, the organization was quickly destroyed, leaders were arrested or fled to the Soviet Union (where some of them perished in Stalin's Great Purge), and thousands of the rank and file disappeared into concentration camps.

2

Poland

Enthusiasm amongst European socialists and radicals for Polish independence had helped to form the First International. Yet, ironically, in Russian Poland revolutionary Marxism gained strength from a revulsion against insurrectionary patriotism. Marx and Engels, obsessed with the international balance of progressive and reactionary forces, hoped that a national rising in Poland would hasten the collapse of the ramshackle Tsarist Empire, thereby hindering Russian intervention against revolution in the West. Many Polish Marxists had a different view of their international duty. The first important revolutionary socialist party in Poland, Proletariat, was established in 1882. One of its leaders Ludwik Warynski, said that 'there is a nation more unfortunate than the Polish nation – the nation of proletarians'. He and his supporters saw no advantage in subordinating the interests of the workers to those of the nation, they believed that in any case the insurrectionary tradition had expired in the disaster of 1863, and placed their hopes for the liberation of the working class in both countries on solidarity with the Russian revolutionary movement. This discord between the masters and their wayward disciples had already rung out loudly in an exchange of messages on the fiftieth anniversary of the 1830 rising. 'The old slogan *Vive La Pologne* has now disappeared completely in the class struggle', wrote the future leaders of Proletariat. 'Poland's services to the European revolutionary cause', retorted Marx and Engels, 'are unforgettable: let us repeat the old slogan *Vive La Pologne!*'

The Social Democratic Party of the Kingdom of Poland and Lithuania, founded in 1893, carried on the anti-nationalist tradition of the first Proletariat. Logically, the Party set itself against the creation of a single Polish socialist movement, sought a close alliance with Russian socialists, and urged socialists in the other parts of divided Poland to collaborate with their German and Austrian comrades. Several amongst the leaders of the SDKPiL were active in more than one socialist party, and the most brilliant of them, Rosa Luxemburg, played a notable part in German and Russian, as well as in Polish socialist circles. It was she who argued the case against Polish independence most eloquently, and endeavoured to prove that the Congress Kingdom was already economically an organic part of Russia which could not be detached without damage to the interests of the proletariat. This eagerness to forgo nationhood caused friction with Russian socialists, who on their side were reluctant to renounce such a useful tactical weapon as the slogan of national self-determination. The SDKPiL felt a special affinity with the Bolsheviks, but were often critical of Lenin's authoritarianism. These misgivings, however, did not cool their passionate longing for solidarity with the Russian proletariat. For his part Lenin, though often exasperated by Rosa Luxemburg's ideas, never lost his admiration for this revolutionary 'eagle'.

Anti-nationalism considerably reduced the appeal of the SDKPiL to the Polish people at large. Its chances of attracting peasant support were particularly poor. While Lenin was preparing to exploit the revolutionary potential of land-hunger, the agrarian policy of the SDKPiL was obstinately orthodox, envisaging the immediate and total abolition of individual farming. Other socialist groups (the Polish Socialist Party – PPS – founded in 1896 and its more radical offshoot, the Left PPS) with a concern for national independence or at least autonomy, in spite of their own divisions and difficulties, commanded more steady support amongst workers than the SDKPiL: while the peasants looked to parties promising land reform. The upheaval of 1905 offered rich opportunities to Polish revolutionaries (the first rising of armed workers in the Russian Empire took place in Łódź in June) but the SDKPiL was too weak to capitalize on them: nor did it draw a lesson from the rapid fusion of revolutionary and patriotic passions among the common people.

In the autumn of 1918, when the collapse of all three imperial powers in rapid succession permitted the establishment of that Polish state which it had never wanted, the Polish Communist Workers' Party (founded in November 1918 from the SDKPiL and some sections of the Left PPS) was at a hopeless disadvantage. It called for the rejection of the independent Polish government and the seizure of power by workers' and peasants' soviets: but where workers' councils were set up they were either dominated from the start by 'patriotic' socialists, or passed into their hands after a brief struggle with the Communists. The elections to the Constituent Sejm in January 1919 were a resounding declaration of popular support for the ideal of independence, and the new government quickly sealed its alliance with the masses by a programme of social reforms and preparations for land redistribution. There was little response to communist calls for seizure of the land. Indeed, it is doubtful whether Leninist tactics could ever have succeeded with the Polish peasantry, most of whom, though poor, owned their land. A shrewd Polish communist told his Soviet comrades that 'if you had our peasants you would have stuck at February (i.e. the February 1917 revolution) and never reached October'.

The prospects of Polish communism were not improved by the Polish–Soviet war of 1920. The Poles were intent on expansion to their pre–1772 boundary, and on creating an independent Ukrainian state as a buffer between themselves and Russia. They also, however, believed that they were preventing an inevitable Soviet attempt to clear the way for assistance to the impending revolution in Germany. Soviet propagandists fed their fears: it was Karl Radek, born in Poland, who first posed the question, later reiterated by Trotsky, whether Poland was to be 'a bridge or a barrier' for the forces of world revolution. After their initial successes, including the capture of Kiev, the Poles were rolled back deep into their own country, and the decisive battle was fought on the approaches to Warsaw. However we explain the Red Army's failure, there is no doubt about the furious heroism of the half-starved, ragged and ill-armed Polish army, the detestation of the Polish population at large for the Russian 'liberator' and their scorn for the group of Polish communists waiting in Białystok to emerge as the provisional government of Poland once Warsaw had fallen.

After the Polish victory before Warsaw, and the agreement on the Soviet–Polish border reached at Riga in May 1921, the Polish Communist Party at last, and reluctantly, brought itself in 1923 to recognize the existence of the new state. In their self-examination after 1920 the leaders of the Party admitted a certain passivity resulting from excessive reliance on the Red Army, and began to contemplate a new approach to the peasant. In the new Poland there was no lack of issues for them to exploit – nightmarish inflation, massive unemployment, the slow and half-hearted implementation of land reform. The Party, however, struck root only feebly in this rich soil. Its leadership was depleted – Rosa Luxemburg and Jogiches had perished in Germany, and many other prominent personalities had passed into the service of the Soviet state (like Dzierzynski and Unszlicht) or of Comintern (like Radek) and its membership remained small. There was never more than a handful of communist deputies in the Sejm, most of whom had defected from other parties after election. In the Eastern borderlands the Party made some headway by playing on anti-Polish feelings among Belorussians and Ukrainians, and the yearning of some of them for reunion with their brothers across the Soviet border. But amongst the Poles fear and hatred of Russia was an insuperable barrier to the spread of communism. Soviet policy in the twenties did nothing to allay Polish anxieties. The Soviet Union, even after the setbacks of 1918–23, still placed great hopes on German communism. It also, however, derived commercial and political advantages from co-operation with Weimar Germany, and tactfully refrained from approval of Poland's Western frontiers. Fears that the Soviet Union might make common cause with Germany to upset the Versailles settlement, or alternatively try once again to build a bridge to the West on the ruins of Polish independence, reinforced Polish hostility to communism.

Thus handicapped and frustrated, the Polish Communist Party languished even before it was driven underground by Piłsudski (whose coup in May 1926 the Party applauded). None the less, Bolshevization and total dependence on the Soviet Union did not convert the factious Party into a tool which Stalin could regard as fully reliable. In 1937, as a precaution in preparation for an eventual rapprochement with Nazi Germany, Stalin ordered the disbandment of the Party and the liquidation of many of its leading members.

3

Hungary

The leaders of the Hungarian communist revolution were distinguished by a singular cultural background. If Jews appeared numerous among the leaders of the Russian revolution by virtue of their prominence, then among the Hungarians the same effect was achieved by real numbers. The reasons are not hard to find. One quarter of the population of the city of Budapest was Jewish. Fifty-one per cent of the country's lawyers were Jews, as were thirty-four per cent of all authors, sixty per cent of doctors and a quarter of all actors and musicians. Surrounded as they were by a deeply national Hungarian folk culture, this cosmopolitan, intellectual sub-population was orientated towards Vienna for its fashions and ideas, rather than towards its Magyar homeland.

When the Austro–Hungarian Empire collapsed at the end of the war, the component nationalities began to search for their national identities, as well as to strive for national independence. But a great part of the intelligentsia was less concerned with defining Hungarian identity than it was to foster Hungary's affiliation to some greater, international, supranational concept. In this sense Communism, as it presented itself to Europe after the 1917 revolution, was the most appealing ideology.

The Hungarian soldiers who dragged themselves back home from the Eastern Front in 1918 brought with them an awareness that what had taken place in Russia was an important lesson for the subjugated peoples of any ramshackle empire. The chaos to which they returned was set in the framework of a phantom Austro–Hungary, out of which Hungary's national independence must arise. In Russia the people had wrested freedom from their exploiters, and in Hungary the same struggle would have as its aim freedom from alien domination.

But beyond the national issue lay another, no less fateful for the outcome of communist action in Hungary. The workers of Budapest had for some time been well organized in trade unions which strongly conformed to Lenin's prognosis of 1902: they not only had never advanced beyond a 'small improvements' mentality, but had not even attempted to go beyond the city boundaries into the factories of other towns in Hungary. The workers, deeply social democratic in their outlook, were at best not interested in agrarian reform, and this was above all the issue which most profoundly moved the greatest part of the population: the peasants wanted land.

In the face of these obvious signs of a hopelessly unbalanced society, Lenin's optimistic description of the Hungarian revolution, in April 1919, appears pure cant:

> Compared with Russia, Hungary is a small country, but the Hungarian revolution might well play a bigger part in history than the Russian. The experience of the Russian revolution is being taken into account in that cultured country. There they are firmly carrying through socialization, and, thanks to the ground there having been better prepared, the edifice of socialism is being raised in a more systematic and more successful way.

All that Lenin had to go on was the wishful reports sent back to him by Bela Kun, who had joined the Bolshevik party while still a prisoner-of-war, and exchanged views with Lenin on the subjects of communism and the communist revolution. But Kun turned out to be one of Lenin's worst pupils, even though the master described him as a good communist. Unlike Lenin – who it must be admitted warned Kun not to follow the Russian example slavishly – Kun could not find it in his heart, still less in his mind, to give the land to the peasants who were asserting their claim to it by the traditional methods of riot, arson and general mayhem. Kun's line, on returning to Hungary in late 1918, was to make a direct bid for leadership of the massive movement of unemployed, strikers and demonstrators by means of resounding promises similar to those which had brought Lenin to power in 1917, but Kun's promises differed from Lenin's in that they were unrealizable. Lenin could after all let the peasants grab the land, and he could after all end the war by not fighting it. Freedom is perhaps a flexible term, open to interpretation, and the supply of bread could be shown to depend on the peasant. Kun, however, promised large wage increases to the workers and big pensions to demobilized troops, whereas it was not within his reach to fulfil such ambitious promises, which obviously depended upon economic recovery and reorganization of the country's resources.

Shortly after the demise of the old regime, in October 1918, the new Hungarian Republic had come into being under the leadership of Count Michael Karolyi, a distinguished champion of Hungarian national independence. But, to an even greater extent than had been the case in Petrograd in the summer of 1917, the republican government relied upon the sole organized section of the urban population, the social democratic party with its working class rank and file, for its support and power. No group, however, was strong enough to resist the humiliating inroads being made upon Magyar territories by the French military occupation, threatening the fragile integrity of the new state. The frustration generated by this situation aroused among the old military and elements of the bureaucracy ideas of alliance with Bolshevik Russia to resist the renewed threat from the West. It was to this bellicose section, as well as to the angry and deprived mobs and unemployed workers, that Kun made his incompatible promises in 1919, and it was they who convinced themselves that he could mean what he said. On the wave of this nationalist socialist dream, Karolyi and his government were pushed aside, or as Lenin put it, 'went into voluntary retirement', and asked Kun, then in prison, to take up the reins of power. They were giving him the rope to hang himself.

In a hastily formed coalition with the social democrats, Kun established the Hungarian Soviet republic in March 1919, at the moment when Comintern was actually being formed in Moscow. The delegates to the Comintern Congress were much encouraged by the events taking place in Hungary: this could easily be the first stage of the greater socialist revolution which would be ignited throughout the old Austro–Hungarian, and no less momentous, the old German Empire, France, England – the world!

Lenin immediately began to assert the authority of Bolshevik experience, especially in the question of alliances. Kun, however, was not free to follow Lenin's strictures on making alliances. Kun's militant promises had led him to the place where the liberals of the Karolyi government were only too eager to leave him to face the national crisis for them. The unacceptable demands being made by the French military commission were expected to arouse the spontaneous protest of the people who, led by the dispensable

Communists, would, it was hoped, march against the foreign foe. In view of the social democrats' power base among the workers, and the communists' lack of a power base in any sector, a merger of the two parties was Kun's only path.

The introduction of socialist-draconian methods into private trade, commerce and industry had the obvious effect of drastically cutting economic activity, thus worsening the overall position. Inflation set in, while simultaneously, fertile Hungary was faced with her first famine. In the midst of these misfortunes, Kun led his people to fight against the Roumanians, who were empowered by the Entente to enter new Hungarian territory. War for the Hungarian communists had come to represent the exact opposite of what it had meant for the Russian Bolsheviks; while Lenin had campaigned to get Russia out of the war and thus achieved power, Kun sought to maintain himself in power, by taking Hungary to war.

Military reverses, Red terror, White terror, peasant uprising, bloody repressions, and war weariness drove many of Kun's rank and file back to the socialists who, before the country was bled white, had begun to campaign for peace. In June 1919 the social democrats all but rose against the communist leadership. The government's requisition policy in the rear undermined army morale; its relinquishing of territory gained by the blood of the troops sent many over to the side of the White enemy. The vast new bureaucracy which nationalization had spawned had brought back to service the old corrupt administration and all the old hatred of this class was reawakened.

Attacks on the government proportionately increased in frequency and violence, as did retaliation. Once the army had dissolved nothing could stop the Roumanians from advancing on the capital, and as Kun had been utterly deserted, the workers would not fight. On 1 August 1919 Bela Kun declared to the Soviet: 'Now I realize that we have tried in vain to educate the masses of the proletariat of this country to be selfconscious revolutionaries'. Instead, the workers were shouting 'Down with the Soviet dictatorship'. Kun immediately abdicated, secured a safe conduct out of the country, ditching some of his most loyal henchmen in the process, and left the Hungarian communists to face the fierce hatred of Bolshevism felt by the masses. This was the moment when the Whites could capitalize on the fact that so many of the Communists, in Hungary and Russia alike, were Jews. Pogroms served to vent popular rage, and reunite the Magyars against the alien force that had so nearly destroyed Hungarian independence.

As for the communist leaders whose brief power was snuffed, they fled for asylum to the place that would serve for twenty years as the guesthouse of communists from all over the world, and then for a short spell as their purgatory – Moscow. Until the Second World War, the Hungarian communists contributed little to the cause of world communism beyond a number of cosmopolitan commissars and agents who could at least claim to have spiked conversation in the Comintern milieu with some racy and eccentric wit. They were unique among their brethren for having, within the few months of their political power, erected the only nude statue of Marx in the communist world. It was a joke which surely only the sophisticated non-Magyars of Budapest could share.

4

Italy

In Italy the combination of a long syndicalist tradition in the labour movement, a predilection for direct action, rooted in the revolutionary reputation of the intellectuals since the *Risorgimento* in the middle of the nineteenth century, and a wide-spread attitude of passive opposition to the war, augured well for communist prospects. If the Russian Bolsheviks could be distinguished by a single characteristic from other parties preaching socialist revolution, it was surely their readiness to act and to take risks, even make mistakes, but above all to eschew the cautiousness which, in a revolutionary situation, could let an opportunity slip through the fingers. In the Italian socialist movement, which like others suffered splits during the war, and which faced the post-war problems with no greater assurance than others, Bolshevik decisiveness, indeed Bolshevik revolutionary success almost alone, appealed strongly to the urge for direct action.

This urge was best expressed and best integrated into a system of ideas by Antonio Gramsci. Of middle class origin, graduate of the University of Turin, Italy's industrial centre, Gramsci conceived of the struggle for socialist reorganization of the state solely in terms of proletarian action. Like Lenin, Gramsci believed that the workers deluded themselves by conducting their trade-union activities within the legal framework dictated by the capitalists. If the ultimate historic mission of the working class was fundamentally to alter the structure of social relationships, then the process could only be started at the heart of the present system, namely, the factory, in which both the capitalist and worker were engaged in the mutual make-believe of 'improving the worker's lot'. From mid-1919, Gramsci began to propagate in his paper *L'Ordine Nuovo* (*The New Order*) the notion of workers' control of the factories. The workers must simply take over their places of work, they must run them and control them in every

7 Genoa Conference 1922. Chicherin (top hat), Radek (bowler),
Litvinov (gloved) – Soviet diplomats on show abroad

8 Moscow street scene mid-1920s. Stalin, Rykov, Kamenev, Zinoviev
parade wardrobe of old Bolsheviks and new leadership

9 In search of new friends. Khrushchev and Bulganin visit India 1955

10 Baku 1920, Congress of Eastern Peoples' liberation movements. Tom Quelch amid fighters against British imperialism

11 End of Chinese 'unity'. Nationalists massacre Communist leaders 1927

detail. Only then would they genuinely be in the position of controlling their own fate.

The success of the Bolshevik Revolution and the founding of the Communist International had immediate and positive response among the Italian socialists. Within the socialist party a small communist group formed with the purpose of carrying out Gramsci's views in practice, by means of party committees inside the factories established on a strictly centralized and disciplined basis. Out of this organization came the formal establishment of the Italian Communist Party.

Italy had emerged from war economically shattered. The discontent which during the war was expressed in pacificism changed after the war to violent outbreaks of all kinds. By late 1919 the peasants, desperate in their near-feudal condition, began to seize and redistribute the land without waiting for state instituted agrarian reforms. A great wave of strikes swept the country, mainly for better pay and conditions. Unrest among the troops had created a sense of impending revolution by the summer of 1920. The time seemed ripe for a test of Gramsci's theory of take-over of the factories as the first phase of the socialist revolution. From a different point of view, the occupation of the factories was an attempt by the Italian workers to make the best of a bad job, since their massive strikes had provoked the employers into locking them out, thus turning the tables. Forcibly to occupy the factories, and then to run them, exactly fitted Gramsci's doctrine of taking the whole question of labour relations and negotiations out of the hands of the capitalists.

The occupation of the factories, however, was carried out in a political vacuum. In spite of the fact that the Italian socialists had emerged as the strongest party in elections of the previous year, and despite the fact that the government and the employers were plainly shaken by the widespread unrest throughout the country-side and among the urban workers, a lingering habit of compromise and conciliation effectively emasculated the serious threat that the events of 1920 might have posed to the state.

The movement was also undermined by the quick cutting off of vital services to the factories. In order to sustain itself the movement had to choose between revolution and seizure of the sources of supply, or total capitulation. The unions, constituting the main force of the movement, were all against taking further action: the seizure of the factories had not brought the government to its

D

knees, a revolution had not been made, and furthermore they had not been psychologically prepared to stage more than one act of the drama. In view of this, the leaders of the Socialist Party, and of the communists within it, were also divided, resulting in the union leaders' beginning to talk with the government.

The government had not intended to confront the workers with force. The prime minister, Giolitti, admitted that there was not enough of it to do the job, and what there was he could not trust. Reaction against the communist threat and repression of the militant labour movement, however, came from another source of power then ascendant in Italy. During the war, the socialist Benito Mussolini had gone over to the side of patriotism, and he now led a growing force composed mainly of ex-servicemen who felt rootless and abandoned, much in need of a cause, but a cause firmly identified with a single man of action. Like the Freikorps in Germany, or the Black and Tans in Ireland, frustrated ex-soldiers called Fascists were looking for a new fight.

If Italian socialists looked to Soviet Russia as a source of strength and inspiration, and if the small group of communists envisaged a new order arising out of the workers' expropriation of the means of production, then there were at least 300,000 strong-arm Fascist Blackshirts under the bombastic leadership of Mussolini who were prepared to challenge them for the role of architect of the new Italy. Against the choice of communism or democracy, the Italian Fascists posed another alternative. The Communists and Socialists were the primary target of the Fascists, but the Fascists were not their only problem, not to say enemy.

The Italians who had gone to Moscow for the Second Congress of Comintern in 1920 returned home with divided minds. The collapse of the movement and the bleak outlook for revolution in Italy were difficult to reconcile with Comintern's demands for stricter alignment with Moscow. Moreover, the Italians, like the French and indeed all other parties, had now to deliberate upon the Twenty-One Conditions of Comintern membership which had been drawn up at the Second Congress. Having lost their chance for revolution, they were extremely reluctant to set about making the split in their own ranks which the debates must generate, especially as it was now obvious that the unions would reject the Conditions.

Pressure was put on them by no less a figure than Lenin

himself, who in November delivered one of his characteristic diagnoses. Of Serrati, who had been present at the Second Comintern Congress and who was seeking ways to preserve the mass trade-union character of the Italian Party, Lenin remarked that he was afraid to destroy the trade unions, the co-operatives and municipalities. The perplexed Italian communists were, according to Lenin, afraid that the reformists, whom they were enjoined to split from, would sabotage their revolution. In effect, Lenin attempted to make the communists understand that not only could they manage without the socialists of mass persuasion, but that they must. Serrati, like Lenin, was obsessed by the single idea of keeping a flexible policy. This Lenin conceded was self-evidently correct. But Serrati was leaning to the right, whereas 'in order to carry the revolution through successfully and defend it the Italian party must again *move somewhat to the left*'. At this point Lenin seems to have abandoned all political or social logic, since he parenthetically also warns the Italians that in moving to the left they must not 'tie their hands nor forget that subsequent circumstances may very well necessitate a certain amount of moving to the right'.

Whether his imagery came from chess or ballroom dancing, it was singularly simplistic as applied to the dilemma facing the Italians. Their revolutionary action had failed, the workers as a whole were uninterested in proletarian internationalism, the Fascists were in open warfare against socialism, and now Lenin was telling them that 'you cannot hope to defend your revolution as long as you have in your ranks reformists and Mensheviks [*sic!*].' Buttressing his argument from historical authority he cited the Russian and Hungarian experiences as examples of this truth. In the Russian case it may well be that the Bolshevik Revolution could not have been 'defended' had there been Mensheviks in the ranks of the party (Kamenev and Zinoviev notwithstanding) but it was an absurd argument. Of the Hungarian revolution, the kind of socialists rank and file was irrelevant insofar as they were not outright nationalists, not to say chauvinists and antisemites. If this was Lenin's intended meaning, he did not make it clear, and it is questionable whether the Italians were in any case able to decipher the Russian symbolism of his terminology. Be that as it may, his object was clear enough: to form an Italian communist section of the Third International which would quickly learn to interpret signals from Moscow without the resistance to be expected from a heterodox membership. Until he came to power it had always been Lenin's primary source of consolation that in time of difficult policy debates one could always split the party, take a high line on principle and go one's own way with a small band of disciples.

At Leghorn in January 1921 the Italians had the opportunity to follow his example. For the delegates at Leghorn it was a bitter irony that none of them wanted to leave Comintern, but neither did they wish to destroy the Socialist Party for the sake of Comintern. As Serrati wrote to Zinoviev after the congress,

> Nobody here wants to leave the Third International, and nobody wants to join the Berne Congress [i.e. the so-called 2½ International, seeking to unite the Second and Third.] If we split it will only help our enemies and our movement will find it absolutely impossible to extract itself from the impasse into which it has been put by the immaturity of the left insurrectionists [Gramsci] and by the diabolical cleverness of Giolitti's government which together pushed us into an unplanned action before we were ready. . . .

All this, however, was merely Serrati's rightward inclination: if anything, it was reminiscent, not of Menshevik attitudes of 1917, but rather of the attitude of the majority of the Bolsheviks, against whom Lenin had had to argue so doggedly, and especially it was reminiscent of the action of Kamenev and Zinoviev, who on the very eve of the seizure of power in November 1917 had openly opposed Lenin's tactics in almost the same words as those now used, after the event, by Serrati.

Moscow's representatives at the Leghorn Congress were to have been led by Zinoviev and Bukharin, but the Italian government refused them visas, and in their place went Matthias Rakosi, a revolutionary tempered in the fire of Hungary, and Christo Kabakchiev, a Bulgarian. Their status was that of plenipotentiaries, that is to say, once launched from Moscow, they had powers to speak entirely on their own initiative but with the authority of Comintern itself. This role of super-ambassador demanded commensurate tact and intellectual authority, an acute awareness of local problems, a respect for the authority and dignity of one's hosts and, for the sake of the parent organization, a capacity for manoeuvre and compromise. It is doubtful whether Zinoviev and Bukharin would have exhibited all of these qualities, but together they might at least have put up a show of tact and respect, affability and intelligence. Rakosi and Kabakchiev did not, however, come from successful revolutionary backgrounds, but rather the opposite. Both were of small mind, to compensate for which they flaunted fiery revolutionary, ultra-Bolshevik attitudes.

The German Paul Levi also attended the Congress and showed greater understanding of his role, but he was no match for the other pair, who made insulting speeches against the majority, referring to them as traitors, social patriots and opportunists. Kabakchiev was especially rampant, but his audience was not slow to react. When he called for the expulsion of the majority, they replied with cries of 'Total excommunication! Vive il Papa! Viva il Papachiev!' And they added, without sarcasm: 'We are not servants, we don't want Papal legates!'

Kabakchiev's line was that the revolutionary situation in Italy was ripe, but that if the workers gave them time to reorganize the bourgeoisie would soon go over to the offensive and the opportunity would be gone to make the revolution a success. In effect, to vote for the Twenty-One Conditions and adherence to Comintern had come to mean to vote for militant action in the streets, when it was already clear that the unions wanted no more, and when the Blackshirts were only waiting for a fight. Acting for Comintern, the plenipotentiaries would not countenance compromise. The Conditions were by now holy writ and the Congress had no choice but to vote. The communists achieved just over one third of the votes, Serrati's centrist position was supported by nearly sixty per cent. Outside the representation at the Congress, however, Serrati enjoyed still greater support among the unions, and as a result of the split at Leghorn the bulk of Italian labour remained outside Comintern, which was thereby deprived of a major though heterodox movement in which it had had the best chance of pursuing its interests.

To argue thus is, of course, to imply that in 1920 the Bolsheviks need not have felt so compelled to formulate the Twenty-One Conditions, whether the compulsion stemmed from revolutionary optimism, as voiced frequently by both Lenin and Zinoviev, or from imminent dysphoria, caused by a presentiment that, if Finland, Hungary and Bavaria had not had successful Soviet revolutions, nowhere else could one legitimately hope to see the proletariat triumph.

5

France

The French socialist party was characterized by, among other things, a strong and long pacifist tradition which survived through the war and which was intensified by the fact that France had herself been the major scene of suffering on the Western front. The mutiny of French units in the spring of 1917 bore witness to the extreme war-weariness and disaffection of the armed forces. The news gleaned by the French troops of the situation in Russia in the summer of 1917 made its greatest impact over the issue of the Soviet demand for an immediate peace without annexations and indemnities. It was Lenin's strident commandeering of this call, rather than the revolutionary corollary of civil war, which captured interest among the demoralized French soldiers and sailors.

In addition, pro-Russian sympathy among the French dated back to the 1890s, when Russian foreign policy underwent a major shift away from its earlier German orientation to a pro-French one. With the fall of Nicholas II and the eventual emergence of a new regime committed to democratic and republican ideals, the Russian ally seemed closer still. Therefore, French intervention against the Bolshevik regime in 1919, however motivated, aroused the strongest hostility among sections of the French forces. In particular, the soldiers and sailors of the French Fleet in the Black Sea, which bombarded Odessa and Sevastopol, eventually revolted at being used against the workers' republic. Severe disciplinary measures ensued, and became a *cause célèbre* at home.

Paris was accustomed to a degree of street violence on May Day, but in 1920 this day of traditional labour protest and celebration seemed to augur wider ramifications. The unrest among the workers, which combined economic discontent with demands for social equity and change among the militant, organized members of old soldiers' associations, culminated in national strikes on the railways, in the docks and throughout the French transport system. Among the members of the old soldiers and ex-prisoners' associations were many who would later figure prominently in the French Communist Party. Their wider interest was anticipated by the new socialist prime minister, Millerand: 'Those in direct communication with the Bolsheviks in Russia judged that this was the moment to turn a widespread strike into the revolution they hoped for in our country.'

But there was no revolutionary strike in France. Instead, communist aspiration found its expression in the founding of the French Communist Party at Tours in December 1920.

The Third International functioned in French socialist history as the wedge which, after the smoke of war had cleared, would split latent opponents in the old socialist parties into those who would seek change and socialism with their own resources, and those who wanted to make their socialist party a local battalion of the world revolutionary army, of which the GHQ was in Moscow. The conflict between these two camps, especially in Eastern and Central Europe, took the form of a conflict over nationalism. In Western Europe, by contrast, the conflict lay more in differences over the kind of organizational structure, trade union policies, parliamentary attitudes, which the party in question might have to adopt should it decide to affiliate with the Communist International.

At Tours the duality of French socialism became manifest and resulted in the formation of the French Communist Party. Leon Blum, who dominated the meeting's social democratic minority, cogently argued that the aims of French socialism were quite alien to those of Comintern. Blum bade the delegates to open their old party cards and to read there the party's aim, which was the transformation of the economic system. He contrasted this with the aim printed inside the new Communist Party cards issued in Moscow: 'The Communist International has as its aim the armed struggle for the overthrow of the international bourgeoisie, and the creation of an international Soviet republic, which is the first step on the way to the total suppression of all government.' This, according to Blum, revealed the essentially anarchistic nature of the Communist International, and thus its profoundly alien character for true socialists.

Blum's argument, like that of his counterparts in other Western European countries where the socialist labour movement had tenacious roots, merely served to identify the 'reformist, reconstructionist' dustbin of history into which true communists were enjoined to cast such bourgeois agents.

Blum's arguments at Tours reflect the deep difference of philosophy that divided the communists not only from the French Socialists but in effect from any other political formation based more or less on the principle of its own freedom of decision. The debate had been gone over ad nauseam among the Russians since the turn of the century, when Lenin systematized the Russian predilection for centralized organization. In 1903, when the Russian Social Democrats split into Bolsheviks and Mensheviks, Trotsky (nominally a Menshevik) described the Leninist scheme in terms which Blum would repeat almost verbatim in 1920. 'The party organization,' prophesied Trotsky, 'takes the place of the party; the central committee takes the place of the organization and finally "dictator" takes the place of the central committee.' Blum added that under these circumstances the dictatorship of the proletariat 'is no longer merely a temporary dictatorship which will allow you to put the finishing touches to the construction of your society. It is a stable system of government which you regard as almost normal, and under the shadow of which you want to do all your work.'

This was a clear echo of the old Menshevik arguments against Lenin's mode of organization, which combined an anarchist approach with one of strictly ordained hierarchy, and excluded autonomy for the lower echelons of the party.

It would be mistaken to suppose, however, that the French socialists who adhered to the Third International were eager to embrace the Leninist mode, especially in their own relations with the central apparatus of the Comintern. Some saw in affiliation to Comintern a potent source of new energy which would indeed restore the defunct structure of the socialist International. Equally, the Bolsheviks were not under the illusion that the French communists would be transformed overnight into disciplined Leninists: for them, Western European affiliations meant wider and more significant areas of possible acceptance and support for the Soviet Republic. Poor tactics on the part of Comintern, however, reduced this potential considerably. On the fourth day of the Tours Congress, at a time when some compromise and unity between the diverse groups was still feasible, a telegram arrived from Moscow signed by the Executive Committee of the Communist International, headed by Zinoviev. In it, the leaders of

Comintern praised the position being taken at the Congress by some delegates, and condemned as reformist that taken by others. The telegram closed by enjoining the former to strengthen their true Communist Party by throwing out all reformists and semi-reformists. In other words, from its inception, the French Communist Party was expected to derive its initiative and momentum from Moscow.

Zinoviev's 'pistol-shot' aroused doubts even among adherents of Comintern at Tours, who none the less favoured joining if only because, in spite of all anxieties, the essential basis for common action in the future must reside in the new international movement.

D*

6

Great Britain

When Lenin, at the end of the 1890s, attacked the prevailing trend among Russian Social Democrats as 'economist', it was from the experience of the English labour movement that he drew his evidence. The trade union movement in England was relatively strong and highly developed, but it was virtually immune to infection by the revolutionary bacillus that was necessary, in his view, to transform it into a *revolutionary* labour movement. The workers organized themselves, and where their champions were of middle class, intellectual origin, they were in most cases still remote from Marxism, had not abandoned their class standpoint, and thought in terms of improving the worker's lot without structural political change.

As everywhere else, the First World War catalysed the latent differences among sections of the British socialist movement. Pacificism and internationalism were above all the most dominant features that became more pronounced in those years, and as a corollary, in a multi-national, multi-racial empire, certain sectional interests hostile to the English system as such were also mobilized. But the traditions of trade-unionism, in its Leninist interpretation, were deep and the bulk of British labour manifested its post-war malaise in stronger agitation for better conditions. The loyalty of most British workers to the social democratic, trade union character of the Labour Party was assured. However, the aftermath of the war, the rapidly changing scene in Europe, the break-up of the old empires and the emergence of totally new states, influenced the rhetoric of political debate and enhanced the extremism of the militants.

In spite of the fact that the founders of the Communist International had long dwelt in England, and that England had, as one of the most industrially advanced countries in the world, represented a promising setting for the socialist revolution, Marxism as such had not, as in the cases of Germany or Russia, been incorporated into an organized party but had remained the province of small coteries of intellectuals, who were characteristically concerned with Marx's economic analysis of the capitalist system rather than with his prognostications of its future.

From America around the turn of the century, British labour received the stimulus to find means of change outside the craft-unions and the parliamentary system to which the majority of their leaders remained wedded. Massive waves of immigrants from Europe were being recruited into high-tempo American industry in social conditions which too frequently were reminiscent of those from which they had fled in their countries of origin, and these people represented perhaps the first generation of proletarians suffering from multiple alienation: cultural, linguistic, economic and political. By its very multiplicity the new American 'working class' was, of course, in Marxist terms both classic, i.e. it had no country of its own, and yet was also anomalous, for within it there could scarcely be any awareness of common class interest. Ethnic bonds strengthened as the best defence against the new exploitation, and class awareness withered as a consequence. None of this, however, deterred the revolutionary Marxist Daniel de Leon from his dream of creating out of this deprived and discontented proletarian mass a great revolutionary organization for workers everywhere, namely the Industrial Workers of the World (IWW). IWW was a New World equivalent of the Socialist International which had the advantage for the British anti-parliamentary left that it preached direct action through industry, and thus offered battle outside both the English political system and the mainstream of the British labour movement.

Although de Leon's ideas had not circulated far nor penetrated the minds of the English workers, among the South Wales miners and the Clydeside ship-workers a number of self-educated Marxists emerged. In 1915 these self-styled Marxists combined efforts to form the Workers' Committee which strongly opposed both the war and industrial peace, which the Labour Party and its trade union leaders had supported. Their success in provoking riots and strikes brought about their dispersal by the government, but this in effect only enabled them to organize their activities on an even wider scale. Among these Marxists were figures who would later emerge as the leaders of the Communist Party of Great Britain, Willie Gallacher, Arthur MacManus, Tom Bell.

The Revolutionary Phase

As in France, there was among the British labour movement a sympathy for the Russian revolution which outweighed suspicions of Lenin's undemocratic methods, and thus there was also in England a strong opposition to intervention in the Russian civil war, opposition much strengthened by the reluctance of servicemen to return to combat in peacetime. The question of joining the newly formed Third Communist International, however, involved only the small Marxist groups, such as the Socialist Labour Party, the Shop Stewards' and Workers' Committee, and the Workers' Socialist Federation. Altogether they could not hope to muster as many as ten thousand, as they were in any case divided fundamentally over participation in parliamentary elections, the very issue which separated them from the Labour movement as a whole.

Parliamentary participation had troubled the Russian Marxists, when the Russian parliament, the Duma, was created after the 1905 revolution. Lenin, in particular, had bitterly observed its divisive effect on the ranks of a small party. Indeed, by the eve of the First World War he had been all but deserted by a significant number of his most able and militant supporters precisely because he pursued a policy of using the Duma as a propaganda platform and as an organizational weapon for internal party fights, despite the fact that he regarded the Duma as a fraud upon the people of Russia.

He saw the British parliament in a similar light, but he also recognized that the need to fight elections would force the small British Marxist groups to unite their efforts and perhaps thus transform themselves into a sizeable Communist Party whose entry into Comintern would be welcome.

The creation of Comintern in March 1919 aroused a strong desire among the anti-parliamentary factions in Britain to become affiliated with this revolutionary organization *par excellence*. But still bedevilled by doubts about impending elections and the fear of remaining an isolated movement, the leader of one tiny group, the ex-suffragette Sylvia Pankhurst, wrote to Lenin in July 1919 to ask his opinion on this vexing question. Lenin's reply to Sylvia Pankhurst was characteristically both practical and opportunistic:

The main thing for any Communist Party is to have a direct link with the working masses, to have the ability constantly to agitate among them, to take part in every strike, to respond to every demand of the masses and especially in England where up to now (as in all imperialist countries) the main participants in the socialist and labour movement have on the whole been narrow elites of workers, worker-aristocrats, most of them thoroughly and hopelessly damaged by reformism, prisoners of bourgeois and imperialist prejudices. Unless there is a struggle against this element, unless its authority among the workers is smashed, unless the workers are made aware of the bourgeois corruption of this element, there can be no serious talk of a Communist labour movement. This is true of England, France, America and Germany.

Coming from Lenin himself, this must have been most gratifying to Miss Pankhurst's sense of her own revolutionary zeal. But Lenin also expatiated on the practical issue facing the British Marxists in a less congenial vein:

But we Russians [prepared the masses for Soviet power by agitation and propaganda] even while we were active in the parliamentary arena. In the Tsarist sham, the landowners' Duma, we were able to conduct revolutionary and republican propaganda. Equally, it is possible and necessary to conduct *Soviet propaganda* inside the bourgeois parliaments.

Thus on balance Lenin made it plain that the British communists (as they were to become) must exploit whatever means were to hand to advance their cause, and that meant, in English conditions, the parliamentary means. He also showed in this letter that from his point of view the significant fact was the imminent choice of fusion or evaporation facing the British Marxist groups, and he therefore counselled unity, not a customary position for him to take.

Personally, I regard a boycott of the elections as a mistake on the part of the revolutionary workers of England, but it is better to make that mistake than to delay the formation of a powerful English Communist Party out of all the groups . . . which are sympathetic to Bolshevism and which sincerely stand for the Soviet republic.

In other words, of utmost priority was support in the West of his own regime and that was most likely to come only through communist parties. Lenin's views were articulated in England by Theodore Rothstein, a Russian Jewish immigrant who also had at his disposal Russian funds with which to aid the publication of organs sympathetic to these views.

The British political arena by 1919 had in fact become extremely agitated, even revolutionary in the eyes of many. Army indiscipline and naval mutinies, a strike of the Metropolitan police, mass unemployment, widespread strikes and deepening discontent were rapidly generating an atmosphere of hostility to Lloyd George's Coalition and in some sectors to the institution of parliament itself. The tocsin was sounded by the Prime Minister himself, when in March 1920 he declared that England could be overthrown more easily than any country in the world and that the crash, should it come, would be greater than in other countries. The socialist revolution was virtually being heralded by none other than the Prime Minister himself! Were the British Marxists preparing to arm the workers and themselves for the occasion, were they helping mutinous servicemen to form Red Guards, and workers to seize the factories? Not at all. The menace of Bolshevism and the spectre of communism were the stilts, fashioned by the British Establishment, on which the midget forces of British Marxism could, unrealistically, have raised themselves up in the summer of 1920, when 150 delegates gathered in the Cannon Street Hotel to form their Communist Party of Great Britain.

Several earlier meetings to negotiate unification had taken place, on the direct initiative of the Comintern from Moscow, and indeed adherence to the Third International had already been decided upon by some of the groups now coming together. In June Sylvia Pankhurst had unilaterally changed the name of her group to the Communist Party (British Section Third International), naturally opposed to parliamentary action and this had prompted the Joint Provisional Committee for the Unity Convention to write to Lenin, as she herself had done, to ask for his opinion on both this issue and that of parliamentary activity and affiliation with the Labour Party, a necessary and painful corollary of such activity. Despite her undoubtedly 'Leninist' method in forming her 'own' party (after which she had promptly left to attend the Second Congress of Comintern in Moscow), Sylvia Pankhurst's action and her line were condemned by Lenin in his reply to the Joint Committee. The policy of parliamentary action was again endorsed, and support of the Labour Party he advised only on the condition that the communists retained their full independence and freedom of action. As he instructed the Italians, in a different context, Lenin tried to steer the British communists into a position which could be seen as politically neutral within left-wing politics in their own country, so long as their open support of Soviet Russia and the Bolshevik regime was proclaimed. The rightward move now, into the Labour Party's orbit, was to be taken with a leftward move at some future time borne in mind. For the moment, unity of the British Communist Party was paramount. The British communists in parliament would, he said, support the Labour Party as the rope supports the hanged man.

His attitude to tactics in bourgeois countries had been fully expressed earlier in the year in his pamphlet 'The Infantile Disease of Leftism in Communism', where he came out specifically against the Pankhurst (and Gallacher) line of seeking total revolutionary means in societies where the best opportunities for revolution lay, clearly in his eyes, within the political institutions of the system.

Although the delegates at the Cannon Street Hotel were barely versed in Lenin's ideas, they adopted his line on the major issue of affiliation with Labour, but no discussion took place over questions of principle affecting the Party's attitudes to the situation in the country at large. Nor was the organizational structure of the new party seemingly shaped by its adherence to Comintern, despite the Convention's evident identification with its Russian ideological leaders.

7

The Peoples of the East

It is perhaps in Lenin's understanding of the revolutionary potential inherent in the colonial relationship that one can best discern
the nature of his 'Marxism'. He had always been impatient with
those who used Marxist teaching as a yardstick to be applied to
the growth of capitalist industry and hence to calculate the
advance of socialism, and he had instead invariably looked beneath the surface of conflict for what might be called the trans-
cendant factors. It may have been wishful on his part to discover a
class struggle in progress among the Russian peasantry, and he
may here have been thinking in terms of the overthrow of the
Tsarist system through nationwide peasant disturbances, rather
than hoping for the socialist revolution to emerge from this
agrarian context. But in the case of the undeveloped colonial
countries he stressed that, beyond the enormous potential of the
drive towards national emancipation, the exploitative connection
between the sources of capital and their colonial interests was,
deep down, the ultimate link in the chain of capitalist history. As
the European markets had returned diminishing profits due to
competition between rival capitalist systems, so the struggle to
control the untapped wealth, in materials and markets, of the
industrially undeveloped countries of Asia and Africa had been
engaged.

The First World War was, in Lenin's view in 1916, the logical
and inevitable outcome of this struggle; it was an imperialist war,
a war to expand and exploit empires made up of subjugated
territories. He further noticed that imperialist expansion had
materially halted the visible signs of impoverishment of workers in
imperialist countries, who thus appeared to have a stake in
colonialism, a stake which helped to explain their patriotism in the
war. At a deeper level, however, it was clear to Lenin that the true
interests of Europe's working class were allied to those of the

subjugated peoples, that is, the overthrow of the capitalist imperialist bourgeoisie.

In this respect, a special role applied to the communist parties of countries most heavily involved in colonial exploitation, especially Great Britain. The non-Russian peoples of the former Russian Empire came under a different category and their position, in terms of self-determination and economic relationships, would be defined within the political structure of the Soviet federation, and without particular reference to the new Communist International. To be sure, the Soviet government would have to weigh in each case the security and economic interest of the, as yet, sole workers' state, bearing in mind the importance of its survival for the World Revolution at large. In Lenin's own view, and constitutionally from 1918 onwards, every nationality of the former Empire had the right of self-determination even should it decide to secede from the new Soviet federation. Where it was plain that secession was a direct threat either to the Soviet economy or security, intervention was justified. Thus in Central Asia, any instability of that area's political integrity both opened the backdoor to Imperialist Britain, always, apparently, poised to pounce out of India – where the British were just as nervously waiting for the Russians to pounce on them – and threatened Soviet Russia with the loss of cotton from Turkestan, or the oil of Azerbaidzhan, as Zinoviev reminded the Petrograd Soviet in September 1920.

Be that as it may, as far as subjugated peoples beyond Russia's borders were concerned, Comintern first faced the problem of formulating revolutionary policy at its Second World Congress in summer 1920, and the area which drew its attention was the Muslim world. The First World War had radically affected the fortunes of the Arab and other populations of that area chiefly through the defeat of the Ottoman Empire. Against the predatory designs of the French and British on the former Turkish lands of the Middle East and indeed of all the lands of the old empire, including Turkey itself, a Turkish nationalist movement of some strength, under Kemal Ataturk, saw as its natural ally the new Soviet Russia. It was above all in Britain and France that Lenin saw the likeliest threat of attack, and therefore he looked to those similarly threatened on his own borders as his first allies. In Turkey he looked to Kemal, in Persia Riza Khan and in Afghanistan King Amanullah. In Palestine Comintern supported Arab anti-Zionism, both because Jewish settlement was endorsed by the British and because Zionist socialism was anti-communist.

The ferment of nationalist revolution in the Near and Middle East, while it greatly reduced British and French hopes of easy expansion, held out little hope for the spread of communism and the formation of national sections of Comintern. Anti-colonialism was not the exclusive province of democratic movements; on the contrary, often it was most effectively expressed by Muslim clergy as well as big landowners, or by the type of military dictator who wished to free his country of this sort of spiritual and economic hegemony, but who would not tolerate the existence of a rival revolutionary party.

For Lenin there was no contradiction in giving support to such regimes, since their primary aim was to overthrow British imperialism, and as such they were bringing instability and revolution nearer in the developed countries of Western Europe. When one of the British delegates to the Second World Congress, Tom Quelch, explained that as likely as not the British worker would view helping the subject peoples to overthrow British rule as treason, he was told by Karl Radek, himself an extreme internationalist by temperament, that the British masses would never free themselves of the capitalist yoke until they had also allied themselves with the colonial revolutionary movement. British communists, he said, would be judged not from the articles they wrote on liberation, but from their number in the gaols of Ireland, Egypt and India, where they must agitate against British imperialism.

Lenin's position was essentially that of the professional revolutionary, prepared to use whatever means lay to hand, be they military dictators, kings, priests or landlords, so long as the main enemy, World Capital, was kept firmly in view. A more theoretical, and certainly more long-term view was put to the Congress by the Indian M. N. Roy, who pointed to the growth of industry in the East as a sign that class warfare was imminent. The Eastern bourgeoisie, he said, and the big landowners, would in due course ally themselves with the Western bourgeoisie against the rising force of the Eastern workers and peasants, and, fittingly, it would be these last two classes which would lead the anti-imperialist struggle. It was therefore the main task of Comintern, Roy concluded, not to help a particular nationalist leader against the Western powers, but to set about the building of communist parties in the East.

The theses on the colonial question, which Lenin had prepared, adopted both Lenin's and Roy's positions. On the one hand the workers of the advanced countries would help those in the backward countries towards the Soviet system and through appropriate stages of development to communism, bypassing the capitalist phase, despite Roy's observations. On the other hand, Comintern would channel this help by means of groups and party organizations in the colonies charged with the task of agitating for peasants' soviets. Analogies of this kind of complex policy are not rare in the history of the Bolshevik Party or of Comintern policy: in 1917 Lenin called for all power to be transferred to the Soviets, while what he had in mind was rule by the Communist Party; in Germany the Soviet regime made an alliance with the Reichswehr against the French, and at the same time planned the overthrow of the same Reichswehr by communism. Similarly, the British communists were enjoined to affiliate with the Labour Party and enter parliament, where they must agitate against both institutions.

Although this approach may be called complex it derived from a simplistic disregard of accidental and personal factors in the particular social contexts. Lenin's dialectical reasoning was faulty in leading him to overlook the possibility that British communists might fail as parliamentary candidates, whether affiliated to Labour or not; or that Kemal Pasha might take his anti-communist feelings so far as actually to kill Turkish communists. So exclusive was Lenin's tactical self-esteem, that he left no room for manoeuvre in response to an opponent's move: he assumed that he was playing both sides.

Almost immediately after the Second World Congress, Comintern organized another meeting which represented a highly original attempt to win support among the Eastern masses for the Soviet system and Comintern. This was the Congress of Peasants and Workers of Persia, Armenia and Turkey convened in Baku. It was chiefly the work of the President of Comintern, Zinoviev, aided by its secretary, Radek, and the recent re-immigrant from Hungary, Bela Kun. In his invitation Zinoviev had asked for 'thousands of Persian, Turkish and Armenian peasants and workers to assemble peacefully for the liberation of the peoples of the Near East'. His address had contained a hint that they would be armed by the Red Army of Russian peasants and workers in order 'to deal with the English, French and American capitalists. Then the riches of your land will be yours.'

Certainly, the Congress was a success if we judge it by the wide range of nations from which delegations came, 1,891 of them from thirty-two Oriental nations, stretching from Morocco to Manchuria, and thus far overflowing the initial intention of the organizers to invite their immediate Near Eastern neighbours only. Two-thirds of the delegates were already communists and forty-four of them were Oriental women.

Despite the wide national spectrum of the Congress, its organizers managed on the whole to stick close to surprisingly obvious areas of vital Russian interest – India, Persia and Turkey, which may have provoked a Turkestani to call upon the Russian leaders to withdraw their colonizers, who were operating in Central Asia under the guise of communism, and to answer in deeds and not merely words the charge made by the West that the Bolsheviks were practising red imperialism among the peoples of Central Asia and the Transcaucasus. This speech must have made a strange impression on Tom Quelch, attending the Congress as a British Communist. In Moscow, he had heard Radek urging the British communists to go among the Irish, Egyptians and Indians and to agitate for the overthrow of the British Empire. In Baku he hears a victim of Tsarist colonialism virtually accusing the Russian communists of carrying on the old tradition under a new name. Why should Irish or Indian workers think otherwise of British communists, than that they were running dogs of capitalist imperialism?

Be that as it may, the atmosphere generated at the Congress by the zealous encouragement of its organizers was one of revolutionary euphoria, which was even then being rendered invalid for some of the delegates by the moves being made by the Soviet government towards treaties as between governments with some of the countries concerned. Thus for instance the Turkish communists, when they returned to their homeland suffused with confidence that their anti-Kemalist revolutionary efforts would be backed by their powerful friends in Moscow, found instead that Moscow placed greater store by an alliance with Kemal, who promptly upon their arrival in Turkey had the Communists suppressed.

Probably the Muslim revolutionaries were misled by the use of

Marxist or Western imagery and took literally the idea of workers' struggle, unsheathing their swords and daggers as they swore, in response to Zinoviev's call, to join 'a Holy War first of all against British Imperialism'. For the only instrument of war established by the Congress was a Council of Propaganda and Action, which appears never to have met, and whose main priority must be judged to have been Propaganda.

The First Congress of the Peoples of the East was also the last of its kind. This lapse on the part of the Soviet organizers is understandable in view of the Soviet government's increasing concern to gain recognition from other states, Eastern no less than Western, and the natural result was an eclipse of the revolutionary, Comintern, component of Soviet foreign policy.

8

China

Lenin said little about Asia and socialist revolution. In addition to seeing the revolutionary potential inherent in the foreign capitalist exploitation of the colonial and semi-colonial countries like China, Turkey and Persia, he had also recognized that in an Asia which lacked a proletariat it could be the bourgeoisie that would lead the anti-imperialist movement. He also saw that such a movement would depend on the mobilization of the peasant masses. As early as 1912, Sun Yat-sen's nationalist platform received Lenin's endorsement as 'truly democratic', but Lenin criticized the Chinese leader for the 'virginal naivete' of his populist would-be-socialism. After 1917 Lenin saw that the communists must give support to this type of nationalism in order to maintain the anti-Western imperialist front.

Until 1920, when the civil war in Russia had largely subsided, there was neither incentive nor possibility for the Bolsheviks to establish contact with the Chinese. Even Marxism had reached Chinese intellectuals only recently, the greater number of them being imbued with Sun Yat-sen's populist beliefs. Moreover, in the virtual absence of a working class the applicability of Marxism could only be expected to emerge after revolution had taken place in Russia, similarly composed overwhelmingly of peasants, a small middle class and a missionary intelligentsia. In 1918 Marxist study groups were formed at Peking University and by May 1919 a number of academicians and other intellectuals had inaugurated a Marxist movement known as May 4th. It included men who were to lead the nationalist party (Kuomintang) and the Communist Party of China, among them Mao Tse-tung. The chief tenets of the May 4th movement, which quickly spread to other centres of intellectual activity, were the cultural rebirth of China, anti-imperialism and social reforms. It is interesting to note that at its very inception the Chinese communist movement had as its object the cultural, literary and spiritual revolution of Chinese society and viewed China's economic problems first of all through the prism of semi-colonialist exploitation rather than class struggle.

The party itself was overwhelmingly composed of students and scarcely a worker was to be found among them. This phenomenon was reflected in Paris in the spring of 1920, when a group of students, among them Chou En-lai, organized a Chinese Communist Youth Corps. This was the component of Chinese communism destined to preserve an awareness of Western thinking and Western developments in the party. Chinese communism began as a small Westernized, culturally reforming element among a starving and demoralized peasantry on whose mobilization the revolution depended. Out of this unlikely class combination emerged the basis of Maoism, according to which communists would bring about a change of attitude in the masses by being among them 'as the fish swims in the sea', but yet maintaining separate organizational integrity.

Despite the nationalist revolution of 1911, China still languished under the semi-colonialist exploitation of foreign concessionaires whose influence was proportional to the military strength of whichever regional warlord they succeeded in patronizing. Political power resided in this military–economic combination. For the communists in China it seemed evident that the socialist revolution could be achieved only by alliance with the peasants, against both the warlords and the commercial bourgeoisie which financed them. In 1922 massive strikes involving railway workers, sailors in Hong Kong and textile workers in Shanghai expressed the combined hostility of the workers for the military dictatorship in Peking and the British exploitation in Hong Kong. The strike committee of Hong Kong together with many workers took refuge from British retribution in Canton, the isolated and uncertain seat of Sun Yat-sen's power. At last his party of intellectuals was offered an opportunity to channel the energies of disaffected workers. In need of advice from the most experienced revolutionaries he knew, Sun Yat-sen made contact with Moscow, and Adolf Yoffe came as envoy to China.

The united front policy then current led to an agreement in August 1922, at a special plenum of the party central committee, that Chinese communists should enter the Kuomintang as individuals, while the Chinese Communist party retained its separate and independent identity.

The KMT was regarded as the party most likely to succeed in completing the nationalist revolution, in driving out the foreigners and overthrowing the warlords. Accordingly in January 1923 the Soviet envoy, Adolf Yoffe, and Sun Yat-sen issued a joint manifesto in which they agreed that while China was not suitable ground for either communism or 'even the Soviet system', Soviet Russia none the less wished to give every assistance to the cause of Chinese national liberation.

Later in 1923 a Soviet team of advisers was sent to Canton with orders to help reorganize Sun's armies and his party organization along Soviet lines. The team was led by Michael Borodin and General Blyukher, veteran of the civil war in Russia. For neither Sun Yat-sen nor the Bolsheviks was this collaboration the paradox it seems: how else should the foreigners be expelled except by their own methods; and how else was the socialist revolution to come except as the inevitable sequel, in countries such as China, to national liberation?

The united front tactics of Comintern and the CCP were viewed with relative equanimity by Sun. He had little doubt that his powerful Kuomintang could deal with insubordination on the part of the adopted CCP members, whose party was still weak in numbers and who were moreover likely to be disciplined by Comintern's wish to stay on good terms with him. Thus Comintern inadvertently encouraged in nationalist leaders an attitude of supremacy towards the communists. It had not been Lenin's intention in his 1920 thesis on the national and colonial question to tie the hands of the communist parties in encouraging the united front tactics. On the contrary, he had expressly stated that they must above all maintain their organizational independence and freedom of action and agitation. His policy was directly taken from Bolshevik experience in pre-1917 days when, as he told the British, the Bolsheviks had successfully carried on revolutionary propaganda from within the arena of the Russian 'landlord' Duma. But, as Lenin failed to see, the situations and the power relationships were quite different. Lenin had wasted years of his and his party's time in making sure that the Bolsheviks did not allow their identity as a group to sink into oblivion by affiliation with the other wing of Russian social democracy, the Mensheviks. How much more of a risk did the Chinese communists take in entering into a party, the KMT, which based its political success and its future on the military and material support of Soviet Russia itself!

In due course the Chinese communists would discover the extent of the risk.

For the time being, however, they believed that they had been affiliated to KMT in order that at some future date they would be in a position to subjugate, if not liquidate, its power. Thus ironically both parties shared a common destructive aim towards each other.

Communist membership of KMT entailed loyalty, or rather avowed allegiance, to two parties, KMT and CCP, each of which was structured à la Lenin on the principle of democratic centralism. This was an impossible position for the communists. Their faith was sustained only by their belief in the ingenuity of the stratagem. In effect the alliance was to bring both parties, by virtue of their combined strength and organization, to the position where either of them could make a bid for total power.

This situation was in fact reached in the spring of 1927. Sun Yat-sen died in 1925 and his successor, Chiang Kai-shek, who had exploited the communist affiliation to build up a strong military force, meant to keep control of the mass movement. The communists for their part had used the opportunities created by the overthrow of the warlords by Chiang Kai-shek to gain followers among the peasants' and workers' organizations in south and central China. The contest between KMT and CCP was thus set in terms of military strength versus popular support. Within KMT itself, however, lay the seed of a long-term problem: as a nationalist party it encompassed numerous socio-political groups which clashed on fundamental issues, such as agrarian reform and the confiscation of private property. Moreover, with so much military strength in many different hands, to take up a political position was fraught with real danger. Wars of various dimensions were an almost continual political background to the struggle between KMT and communists and Left and Right KMT.

The growing influence and self assurance of the communist-led labour movement and the confidence which it in turn inspired in the CCP, aroused alarm in the KMT. A plan by Borodin to make a military expedition to free the north of foreign and warlord domination (a plan projected precisely because Borodin sensed the imminence of clash with KMT) augured further expansion of communist power. But in March 1926, while Borodin was away gathering support for the expedition, Chiang Kai-shek decided to act. He arrested communists in Canton, restrained the Russian military advisers attached to his army and then wrote to Borodin begging him to return, whereupon he explained that although Soviet help was welcome he would not tolerate Chinese communist ambitions. In April 1926, to satisfy Borodin of his good faith, he got rid of extreme right-wing members of KMT.

In Moscow Trotsky and the Opposition voiced increasingly sharp criticism of Comintern policy. The Chinese communists, they argued, must not remain in alliance with the nationalists but must engage in open struggle against them. Stalin, on the other hand, as late as November 1926, stated that it would be a grave error for the communists to leave the Kuomintang. But the decision was not the communists' to make. Chiang Kai-shek's military successes on the Northern Expedition encouraged him to terminate the alliance with CCP, which threatened the hegemony of the nationalists. In April 1927 he staged a coup against them in Shanghai, disbanding left organizations and ordering the execution of thousands of communists and other left-wing militants. A few days later in Peking CCP leaders were executed and the Soviet Embassy was raided.

By now it was evident that Stalin's (and Comintern's) China policy was wearing thin. In May Stalin continued to defend the policy of alliance, and in June the CCP Central Committee passed a resolution requesting the left-wing KMT to oppose Chiang Kai-shek and to carry on the revolution. But by August/September, it was clear that the Chinese communists were being led along a hopeless path. Borodin's leaving China in July only emphasized the bankruptcy of Comintern's China policy. The need to save the CCP by separating it from KMT became urgent. In September 1927 an insurrection was launched in Hunan under the direction of Mao Tse-tung, but it failed, for the KMT/CCP alliance had already vanished. In September Stalin finally conceded the treachery of Chiang, whose party had sold out to the counter-revolution. But in view of Stalin's own position vis-à-vis the Trotsky/Zinoviev opposition, he was careful to maintain a commitment to action in China not conceding defeat. He sent more agents, this time to organize an uprising in Canton where, he argued, a good revolutionary situation existed as the basis for mobilizing the revolutionary peasants of South China.

The revolt was duly launched in December 1927, but it was over in a matter of three days and was followed by another massacre of communists. In July 1928, the Chinese delegate to the

Sixth World Congress of Comintern stated that the Chinese revolution had been defeated for a number of reasons, including the international situation, military intervention by the imperialists, betrayal by the KMT and its class supporters, but above all it had been defeated by the serious opportunistic mistakes committed by the leaders of the Chinese Communist Party. Thus were the Chinese the first of many communists to stand before their comrades, and in direct contradiction to at least some of the true facts, to castigate themselves for failures which in the nature of things could scarcely have been avoided. In the case of China, Soviet help to the KMT was obviously correct when it was decided upon, and so was CCP affiliation, since otherwise the Chinese Communists would have had no protection whatever against the growing power of KMT, and might have undergone the fate of their Turkish comrades years earlier. Time in fact lay at the root of their dilemma: alliances with nationalist parties so strongly endorsed by Lenin had no terminal date set to them. By definition they could be ended only when they had become untenable or intolerable. Where war and military strength are the measure of political compatibilities, the means of terminating the alliance must, as with the Chinese, be disastrous for the weaker.

part 3
The Defensive Phase

1

The Popular Front

The year 1934 was a turning point in the history of Comintern, as in that of the Soviet Union. The emergence of Hitler's militarist expansionism and the plainly imminent threat of annihilation of the German communist movement galvanized Stalin into a series of defensive actions which effectively cut across Comintern's field of operations, setting the stage for a new phase. The 1930s was a time of the great pathologies in Europe, Hitler's insanities being matched in Russia by Stalin's and between them one of the victims crushed was the international communist movement, such as it was.

Stalin however had been slow to abandon his stand against the Social Democrats under his leftist policy. Hitler's seizure of the German trade unions in May 1933, and his burning of the books in Berlin, were not matters of great concern to Stalin, who in January 1934 stated, using the analogy with Italy, where Fascism was not an obstacle to Italo–Soviet relations, that Nazism did not hamper good relations with the Third Reich. Taking courage from Stalin, some of the German communist leaders showed bravado at the arrest of some thousands of their rank and file, claiming, like Heckert, that with 5 million followers the Party need not fear. Heinz Neumann, on the other hand, blamed Hitler's victory on the policy of the German Communist Party, his attack justifiably interpreted as an attack on Stalin's and Comintern's policy. The stubborn, divisive tactics of the anti-Social Democrat platform contrasted grotesquely with the earlier policy of united front, although, in the short term, the results for the German communists would not be qualitatively very different from what they had been for the Chinese communists a few years earlier.

Stalin's attitude toward the Nazis underwent a drastic shift, however, when it became apparent that Hitler's dream of German glory entailed not merely an anti-communist mission to the world, but the incorporation into the Third Reich of a substantial part of

119

the Soviet Union. From the middle of the 1930s, therefore, Stalin's main attention was concentrated on achieving military and non-aggression alliances against Germany's designs. In May 1934, alliances were made with France and Czechslovakia, and in September of the same year the Soviet Union entered the League of Nations, from which Germany and Japan had departed the year before.

The natural concomitant of Soviet foreign demands in Comintern policy was the task of mobilizing support for the Soviet Union at a popular level. After 1934 Comintern operated on what in effect was a united front platform which extended almost indefinitely to include alliances and co-operation with parties that were not only socialist or bourgeois-nationalist, but even conservative. While trying to secure external guarantees of national stability, Stalin simultaneously carried out a massive 'reform' of the Communist Party, Comintern and state apparatuses. Against the background of terror inside Russia, Stalin's 'general line' followed a zig-zag course of bewildering reversals, such as attempts to merge with socialist parties, the dissolution of communist trade unions and their substitution by 'fronts' manipulated by Comintern, and culminating in the greatest political somersault of all, the Molotov–Ribbentrop (Stalin–Hitler) Pact of August 1939.

Within this development, two primary facts of life confronted communists, one made to seem dependent on the other: the proletarian world revolution which had been halted in the 1920s now sank beneath the earth, and Comintern activities henceforth must be in direct support of Russian foreign policy. The new programme was called the Popular Front, first successfully practised in France in 1934 and promulgated officially at the Seventh (and last) Congress of Comintern held in the summer of 1935. Communists were instructed to work together with any elements that were opposed to Hitler, to support rearmament and to cease anti-parliamentary propaganda. To be sure, no abandonment of revolutionism was mentioned. On the contrary, Georgi Dimitrov, chairman of the Congress, pointed out that the policy would enable the communists to enter into the heart of the bourgeois camp with the help of the Trojan Horse. The Popular Front, that is, represented a policy of infiltration and manipulation, a period of preparation for the 'forthcoming great battles of the second round of proletarian revolution'.

A SOVIET SPRAT TO CATCH A MANDARIN MACKEREL

Moscow's manipulation of Chinese
mmunists and Nationalists (KMT)
Western view of united front, 1926

13 Poland's Cyrankiewicz
meets Mao, Peking 1957

Chinese appetite for mass reproduction finds expression on first
iversary of the republic, 1951

15 Pro-Soviet,
anti-fascist parade,
Paris, 14 July 1936

16 Party school,
Paris 1953

17 1930s depression
boosted US
Communists. Earl
Browder (second
right) at election
rally, 1936

Dimitrov's metaphor was not mere mollification, since in France, for example, the merger of the Communist trade unions with others had not represented a change in underlying strategy, for with the Bolshevization of the Party it was the factory cell which effectively transmitted communist influence.

The inauguration of the new line coincided with the intensive amplification of Stalin's personal cult, a necessary concomitant of the massive purges to come; if Stalin was going to make a public show of his struggle against the 'deviators', 'wreckers', 'spies and saboteurs', that is Lenin's Bolshevik Old Guard, then he must, by contrast, be made to seem the very paragon of Marxist–Leninist virtue. The omnipotence ascribed to such a figure would accrue in the process of trials and liquidation as it went on. At the Seventh Congress Stalin was greeted as 'Leader, Teacher and Friend of the proletariat and oppressed of the whole world'.

As never before, the Soviet regime regarded its main task as an exercise in public relations on a world-wide scale, and it was now self-evident that its appeal must be directed to sections of society which would not knowingly endorse communism or avowedly communist aims, but which would support objectives of ultimate interest to the cause of world communism. In a sense this had always been Lenin's approach: it had been implicit in his doctrine of party organization and tactics, as laid down in his *What is to be Done?* written in 1902. There he said that all kinds of peripheral organizations should be exploited if they could at all be to the advantage of the party.

The first attempt to exploit a cause in the interests of the Soviet world image had come during the great famine of 1921. An appeal by the Soviet government drew an immense response in the form of the American Relief Administration, organized by Herbert Hoover, and described by the Russian writer Maxim Gorky as a humanitarian act of unprecedented proportions. The Red Cross had also sponsored a Council for Russian Relief. In order, as it were, to put up a show from the workers of the world, the International Workers' Help (MRP, the initials of its Russian name) had been set up in Berlin by one of the most gifted Comintern virtuosos of the 'front' technique, Willi Münzenberg. The manner in which Münzenberg set about this new venture (he had until then been running his own Communist Youth International) was characteristic of everything he later did. He set up two popular newspapers, a book club and library, organized film shows, both in Russia and abroad. Never losing sight of the MRP's ostensible first aim of collecting material aid, which it indeed accomplished in large measure, Münzenberg added a vital new ingredient to these operations: a sense of commitment on the part of the givers. His great propaganda machine served two functions: first, it generated a keen interest in what was happening in Russia, and second it encouraged foreign workers to identify their contributions with the fact of their being workers, by urging them to give a day's pay, or a quantity of their products. This practice was manifestly valuable in gaining solidarity with the Soviet Union abroad, so much so that MRP was kept going after the famine was over: MRP apparatus, including mobile soup kitchens, were to be seen during later times of proletarian troubles, such as among the German unemployed and during the British General Strike of 1926.

Münzenberg's entrepreneurial flair led him into a profusion of ventures, including illustrated magazines and newspapers, the distribution of Soviet films in many countries, and a network of contacts with banks and commercial establishments, all of which helped party propaganda and earned good money for the cause.

Münzenberg's modus operandi was especially valuable when the Nazi threat began to loom. In August 1932 a peace congress was organized in Amsterdam, which was attended by thousands of delegates. For the sake of maintaining an innocent appearance the congress was directed by the French pacifist writers Romain Rolland and Henri Barbusse. It was followed in June 1933 by the formation in Paris of the World Committee against War and Fascism. Münzenberg realized that the rise of Fascism offered Comintern the opportunity to fight on ideological grounds and that it was therefore essential 'to organize the intellectuals', a process to which innumerable Western intellectuals willingly submitted. It was essential to 'front' tactics that Moscow's interest should not be obvious: political neutrality enhances the morality of any argument. The chairman and committee of a front organization would therefore be politically 'respectable', while their utterances and actions would be guided by the communists behind them. With the noble aims of struggle against Fascism and prevention of war (through rearmament, to be sure), the 'fronts', or 'Innocents' Clubs', as Münzenberg called them, attracted vast numbers of Western professionals, lawyers, teachers, doctors, writers and artists.

An interesting development took place inside the communist movement itself as a result of these highly varied activities. The official, overt parties which had been recast in the image of the master-party, the Communist Party of the Soviet Union, and whose leaders had more or less successfully been modelled to conform to the Leader of them all, continued to function in the customary fashion, heavily handled up and down the hierarchy in accordance with the Leninist system of democratic centralism. This principle signifies that all decisions of the Centre are reached only after full and free discussion of the issue by the lower levels, down to the cells, and that once the Centre has reached and promulgated its decision all members shall diligently carry it out, on pain of disciplinary action by the higher levels. By contrast, Münzenberg's operations were necessarily performed in conditions which left him literally a free agent, expanding and ramifying whenever and wherever the opportunity arose. Uncomfortable among the Russians whom he found tiresome, inefficient and dictatorial, Münzenberg had never felt at home in the Comintern *apparat* as such. Early in the 1920s he had disappointed Zinoviev, then its President, by his lack of discipline, and he had always preferred to create his own milieu. Nor was he felt to be under control in his own German Communist Party, whose Stalinist proletarian leader, Walter Ulbricht, felt antipathy for the cosmopolitan freewheeling of Münzenberg and those around him.

In fact Münzenberg and his set-up embodied the original character of Comintern, the internationalist cosmopolitan, the adaptable polyglot, imaginative and mobile, inhabiting a sector of the Soviet apparatus still left relatively free and, by contrast with the tasks of their official parties, much more interesting to work in. It is therefore not surprising that Münzenberg attracted many communists who found Party life stifling. Münzenberg and his collaborators, however, came to be regarded with growing suspicion by party leaders and by Moscow. Their independence was thought to have arisen from incipient deviations, fed by their relative freedom from discipline.

The promulgation of the Popular Front in the summer of 1935 coincided with the wave of purges of the leadership within the regime, set off by the assassination of Leningrad party leader Sergei Kirov, an event possibly engineered by Stalin himself. Four show trials were staged between August 1936 and March 1938 which, together with clandestine trials, liquidations, imprisonment and deportations without trial, accounted for the effective annihilation of the entire Bolshevik Old Guard, the majority of the armed services' general staff, most of the Comintern upper echelons and apparat, and many of the East European communists who had come to the socialist fatherland as a refuge from Fascism.

The charges brought against those put on trial were immensely varied. One thread, however, is discernible throughout – the charge of foreign contact, conspiracy with outside elements and enmity for the Party supported by foreign powers. In seeking ways to stabilize and strengthen his regime, Stalin exploited the very defect in his political character which in 1922 had caused Lenin concern about his Georgian subordinate, the Great Russian chauvinism of the non-Russian national in the Russian context. Russian nationalism now came to be seen as a safer basis than internationalist revolutionism. Since organized opposition to the regime had clearly been already crushed by Lenin, material or other aid to 'traitors', that is, political oppositionists, had to come from outside and thus inevitably entailed treasonable activity. Needless to say, the entire tragic farce of the trials has been exposed many times over, even by internal evidence, and later by Khrushchev, as well as observers who were present, as a huge fabrication. None the less, the first implication of the horrendous charge was that it must compromise all those whose legitimate Party work brought them into contact with foreigners. To be sure, this would not even exclude such as the Party leader of the Uzbek Republic, Faizulla Khodzhayev, for plainly his anti-Soviet activities were supported by the British, ever-vigilant for an opportunity to expand their Empire at the expense of the Soviet Union, or so it was alleged at his trial.

Over and above those party functionaries whose connection with a national minority of the Soviet Union made them a target for Stalin, the Comintern leaders and *apparatchiki*, or party hacks, were especially vulnerable. Since conspiracy with the exiled Trotsky was a primary charge in all the trials, Comintern agents were systematically recalled to Moscow, where in countless cases they were greeted by a bullet in the back of the neck, or stripped of their identity and carted off to concentration camps as mere numbers, their Party record being of no more value to them than innocence was to the thousands of ordinary Soviet citizens being similarly treated. The arm of Soviet 'justice' did not rest until, in 1940, it finally reached out to Stalin's chief adversary, the biggest fish who had been allowed to escape during the carefree 1920s, Leon Trotsky, who after long and devious attempts by Stalin's agents was eventually assassinated in Mexico.

Trotsky's informed and biting commentaries on Stalin's actions had become a source of growing irritation. As Stalin's policies alienated growing numbers of disillusioned communists, more and more of them recognized the validity of Trotsky's criticisms, though few were actually prepared to ally with him and his meagre Fourth International. Trotsky's criticism of Stalin in effect came down to condemnation of the Leader as a poor custodian of the Soviet state, a wrong-headed, barbaric, dangerous and ill-equipped successor to Lenin for the task of leading the Soviet masses and the world proletariat to communism.

The gradual accumulation of informed communist and ex-communist opinion against his methods, and anxiety about the possible growth of similar opinion in the Soviet Union itself, represented for Stalin an irksome impediment to the freedom he needed to carry through the complex and ideologically acrobatic manoeuvres confronting him in the late 1930s. In order to be able to engage in tactics which effectively would betray many proletarian and revolutionary promises, Stalin had to ensure complete unanimity of official communist opinion. He apparently believed that he could only achieve this aim by striking terror into the hearts of all those within reach at home, whether communist or merely Soviet citizens, while at the same time using the 'front' organizations to manipulate opinion abroad.

The cult of Stalin as the infallible leader and the cult of 'nation' as the means to maintain mass support against the threat to Russia from Hitler, had their appropriate reflections in the national sections of Comintern. In Britain, for example, the communists' hero was Harry Pollitt, whose wisdom and integrity were exalted, while the British Communist Party paraded as the party most strongly opposed to the 'un-British' activities of Mosley's Blackshirts. Elsewhere the same sort of phenomenon was created, the internationalist element in Communism being played down in favour of its patriotic obverse. In the USA, for instance, the Communist magazine *New Masses* ran an essay competition on the theme 'I like America', and at Communist Party meetings henceforth the 'Star Spangled Banner' was played. This development arose from a completely hypocritical and indeed unrealistic

125

policy foisted on the non-Russian parties by Moscow: the basis of Stalin's personal cult was the real and total power that he wielded, and the basis of Russian nationalism lay in the need to defend the socialist fatherland. In the other cases communist leaders had neither the power nor the emotional commitment to rely on, and their posturing merely encouraged their critics.

Against the background of terror, nationalist conformism and non-revolutionary caution, the Spanish civil war erupted as a major acid test of Soviet good faith and communist loyalties. The Spanish labour movement was rooted in a highly revolutionary but non-Marxist tradition, in which anarchism and reformist socialism formed an alliance. Anarchism and violent means of struggle predominated and were poor soil for the growth of authoritarian, centralized Communist organizations, which remained very few and very small, were repeatedly split and lacked mass following.

Socialist co-operation with the Spanish Republic, proclaimed in April 1931, was attacked by Comintern as treason, in accord with the then current left policy. The Communist Party of Spain called persistently for a federated socialist republic based on workers', peasants' and soldiers' soviets, and no alliances with other republican parties. Groups which split from the Spanish Communist Party over this line, including those of Nin and Maurin, combined to form the Workers' Party of Marxist Unity (POUM).

Elections in 1933 restored the fortunes of the right-wing Catholic parties and set in train a wave of unrest and violence. In Madrid an armed march against the Ministry of the Interior was easily crushed by the government owing to lack of unity among the left-wing organizations and the indecision of their leaders. In militant Barcelona a Catalan separatist rebellion, which proclaimed federalist slogans, was similarly crushed, the anarchists of their trade-union allies having held themselves aloof. Outbreaks elsewhere in Spain during that autumn of 1934 were similarly put down by the government. The most momentous clash took place in the province of Asturias, where some 30,000 miners organized a Red Army dedicated to resisting if not attacking the right-wing government. For fifteen days the Soviet of Asturias directed a minor civil war. The miners of Asturias, a highly political group, formed a spontaneous united front with anarchists, socialists and communists, as well as the Trotskyists, the movement as a whole calling itself the Union of Proletarian Brethren (UHP).

For the Spanish communists, united action in Asturias represented a combination of both alliance with other parties and zealous revolutionism. The Spanish socialists greatly admired the Soviet achievements among the peasants and workers in Russia's backward economy, and the communists had, therefore, to take up positions to the left of those advocated by Comintern. The Spanish Communist Party, which rose in numbers from about 3,000 in 1931 to not more than 35,000 at its peak in 1936, boasted few outstanding personalities. One exception was Dolores Ibarruri, Basque by origin, and married to an Asturian miner who helped found the Communist Party in the north of Spain. Ibarruri became famous under her battle-name of La Pasionaria during the Asturias rising when, as a communist, she gained a reputation for her fiery oratory and total dedication. A less colourful figure, but one who by his origins might have secured a Stalinesque position, had the civil war ended differently, was José Diaz, an ex-bootblack from Seville.

The Asturias rising, was cruelly suppressed after bloody fighting and the exhaustion of the insurgents' ammunition, but communist co-operation augured well for the future of the Popular Front in Spain. In February 1936 new elections took place and, at the proposal of the communists, the leftist parties fought under the banner of the Popular Front, though the Communist Party itself won very few seats in the new parliament. This situation arose because the parties of the liberal middle class were more afraid of the Fascists than they were of the left, despite the militancy shown in Asturias. As a result, the Popular Front gained a majority (later disputed on statistical grounds) over the other blocs. The right-wing National Front came second and the centre parties last.

In France the success of the Popular Front during elections which in the previous June had, with the support of the communists, brought the Socialist, Léon Blum, to power, had provoked street clashes between left groups and Fascist organizations. In Spain, a similar outcome to the elections mobilized the Fascist forces under Franco in an armed crusade to tear down the Red Flag, the symbol of the 'destruction of Spain's past and her ideals'.

Stalin's response to the outbreak of civil war in the summer of 1936 could not be a simple one. While he was ideologically committed to victory for the Republic, in which the communists were now an integral part, he none the less had reservations about the possible revolutionary outcome in the event of such a victory. If the Fascists won, then France would be extremely vulnerable on her Spanish, German and Italian frontiers, and Hitler would be correspondingly freer to act against Russia; on the other hand, it was no less vital to Stalin's hopes for an alliance with Britain, as well as France, that communist revolution should not raise its head too high in Spain, for that would compromise the Soviet Union in its dealings with the bourgeois powers. In July 1936, at the same time that Hitler and Mussolini agreed to General Franco's request for military aid, and the French government had been forced by British caution and right-wing opinion in France to grant only indirect aid, a joint meeting in Prague of Comintern and Profintern decided to raise 1,000 million francs for the Spanish government.

The decision to aid Spain was literally the (temporary) salvation of Willi Münzenberg. He had recently been recalled to Moscow and politely questioned about his activities by the NKVD. The outbreak of war in Spain and his possession of innumerable international contacts which could be mobilized in the cause enabled him to persuade Comintern to let him out of Russia. The fate that he managed to elude in 1936 in Russia caught up with him in a French forest in 1940, when he was murdered while escaping from German-occupied France.

Before that final curtain came down, however, Münzenberg staged one of his most successful and extravagant productions: *International Red Help*. A plethora of front organizations came into being in many countries with the aim of collecting aid for the Spanish cause. All the expertise gathered by Münzenberg was focussed on this single target. The aid which was sent was at first, however, in the form of food, money and non-military material. Military aid, in the form of arms, pilots and technical assistance, was eventually wrung from Stalin mainly by the persuasion of foreign communists and by the news from Spain. Nothing was sent, however, until more than half of the Republic's gold reserves, some £60,000,000 worth, had been safely landed by ship at Odessa, serving as both a surety to the Soviet government and a security for the wealth of the Republic.

For Stalin, involvement in Spanish affairs was necessary to ensure that the extremist elements in the Republican forces were not too successful in the installation of revolution. His attention at this time was chiefly engaged in manoeuvring on the plane of *Realpolitik*. As early as 1936 Stalin pursued secret negotiations with Germany in case a pact might be made there, instead of with evasive and reluctant Britain. Therefore, as far as Spain was concerned, Stalin sought to gain a measure of control inside the government. His major target was, naturally, the dissident and Trotskyist elements, who were terrorized, tried and assassinated by NKVD agents specially sent from Moscow. While the Republic battled for survival, and young idealists of the International Brigades watched dumbfounded, Stalin's agents in effect transferred some of the horror of mid-1930s Russian life to Spain. As early as December 1936 the Soviet intention of extending its private war against deviationists had been spelled out in *Pravda*: 'the cleaning-up of the Trotskyist and Anarcho-syndicalist elements has already begun and will be carried out with the same degree of energy as in the USSR'. It was a policy which psychologically prepared many dedicated communists for the greatest betrayal of all, the farthest possible extension of the Popular Front, not against Fascism and Nazism, but alliance with them, the Hitler–Stalin Pact of 1939.

E*

2

USA

From the outset the American Communist movement was beset by factional hostilities arising chiefly from its heterogeneous ethnic make-up. It even began as two parties, becoming nominally one only from 1922. Successive waves of immigrants from Germany, Sweden, Russia, Ireland, Holland and elsewhere, had since the end of the nineteenth century developed their own trade union organizations and mutual aid societies which, as elsewhere, had acquired greater political awareness under the impact of their new country's involvement in the First World War. With few exceptions American trade unions were motivated by the same materialist urge as that which powered the seemingly inexhaustible economy. Even among intellectuals, Marx's dogmas of pauperization and class warfare struck only tenuous root during the time, after the war, when America's prosperity rose steadily. From 1929, however, the picture altered radically, for the great upward sweep of the American economy was in that year suddenly and traumatically reversed and changed into an economic and psychological depression of unprecedented degree. The gilt-edged security of the American financial and industrial structure, until then a standing mockery of Marx's apocalyptic prophecy of capitalist disaster, was overnight exposed as in fact a system no less in the grip of the anonymous iron laws than any in Europe. In the 1930s Marx's interpretation of social development suddenly acquired validity and veracity for a generation of American intellectuals.

In political terms, the rise of Fascism and its growing bellicosity in the mid-1930s awakened American liberals to Soviet pacifism. The promulgation in 1936 of Stalin's new Soviet Constitution, a paragon of democratic virtues, lent credibility to a nascent idea among American liberals that the Soviet Union was the sole and most reliable defender of the spirit of freedom and democracy in face of capitalist senescence and fascist brutality. Russia moreover appealed to American reformists who had become dismayed by the vicissitudes of the free market economy which clearly terminated in the great depression. Planning, economic and social, emerged as the sane alternative to the reckless *lassez-faire* of the American tradition, and furthermore it was in accord with the New Deal proclaimed by Roosevelt, and ideally suited to the new Comintern policy of the Popular Front. In other words, wide sectors of intellectual opinion in America were coming halfway towards the communists. The 1930s represent the most dynamic, if also hectic, period of the American Communist Party's history.

Intellectual admiration for the Soviet Union was tacitly approved by the long-delayed diplomatic recognition accorded by the USA to the Soviet Union in 1933. Maxim Litvinov, the Soviet foreign minister and one of the very first Bolsheviks, toured the US with his daughter, making a good impression of civility and cordiality and in general softening the image of the USSR in the eyes of ordinary Americans.

In effect, communism arose to its greatest strength in the US not as in some European countries during a revolutionary period, but at a time when national need coincided with Stalin's non-revolutionary line, and thus American communists were most active in favour of national unity.

Having somehow survived the antagonism which had existed between the ethnic, especially the Russian-Jewish, and the 'American' (that is, Anglo-Saxon) groups during the 1920s, the Communist Party in the 1930s was subjected to far greater stresses by the somersaults of Soviet and Comintern policy. The same was of course true of all other national parties, but the American Party was especially vulnerable, first because it failed to gain ground among the organized trade unions, but perhaps more important also because, having drawn in so many writers, journalists and professional intellectuals during the great depression, it was too well endowed with commentators on policy. Indeed it can be said that multiplicity and defiant expression of opinion was the national characterizing hallmark of American Communism, stemming perhaps from the same tradition in American history as the democratic process itself. For this reason it is logical that Trotsky should have found the most articulate and probably the largest following among American communists, for if nothing else by the

1930s Trotskyism had come to represent cogent communist criticism of Soviet policies, couched in terms of intellectual truth and honesty against Stalinist lies and deception.

The American Communist Party probably had the greatest voluntary turnover in membership of any party, mainly as a result of its many intellectuals. Having during the depression recruited so successfully in the universities, the membership was extremely volatile at times and there were frequent changes of line. Small magazines and newspapers proliferated, so much opinion needing expression. The ever-present tendency among intellectuals to mock at hypocrisy was over-stimulated by Stalin's policies and one consequence that has been well documented was the heavy borrowing by the CPUSA leadership, under Earl Browder, from the American tradition of anti-intellectualism, a conscious attempt to 'put beef' into the party's over-articulate intellectuals, to teach them discipline, in other words to quieten them down somewhat. But this approach met with little success, for being above all men who had espoused communism the doctrine, rather than the Communist Party, they were in large measure prepared to leave the Party when put under pressure. Discipline was always weak in this sector. To be sure, many, more than elsewhere, also dropped communism upon leaving the Party, and certainly no other party has generated so many vocal and dedicated anti-communists as has the American Communist Party.

However, the Party itself was not devoid of versatility, and 'front' organizations were especially prolific in the United States, where the abundance of social organizations attendant upon the economic and social dynamism of the system provided ideal soil for such operations. Possibly the Party's greatest feat was its disappearing act in 1944. Consumed by the euphoria created at Teheran by the expressions of eternal amity from Stalin and Roosevelt, the American Communist Party leadership unanimously decided to dissolve itself. Under the slogans of 'End the War' and 'Open the Second Front', a new organization was thereupon formed, calling itself the Communist Political Association and rallying anybody who would listen to the banner of the 'National Front', extending fom the poorest Southern negro to the biggest bourgeoisie. It was from this scattering operation that Senator Joe McCarthy was later able to glean sufficient evidence of infiltration into government agencies and elsewhere to terrorize and persecute the American intellectual world, and for once it may be that the local product proved more damaging to the tradition of freedom of speech and conscience than even Stalin could manage in America.

3

European Communism during the Second World War*

Within hours of the German attack on the Soviet Union on 22 June 1941, the Comintern sent telegraphic appeals to all those Communist Party Central Committees with which they were in contact. In the case of the Yugoslavs the text, which has survived, read

It is vitally necessary to develop a movement under the slogan of a united national front for the protection of the people subjugated by Fascism. Such an exploit is indissolubly connected with the victory of the USSR. Bear in mind that at the present stage it is a matter of liberation from Fascist subjugation, and not of socialist revolution.

The Soviet Union had long ago arrogated to itself the sole right to assess the prospects of revolution in other countries, and to determine the tactics of individual communist parties, which were merely sections of the Communist International in Moscow.

Past experience of spontaneous revolutions with nominal Soviet support – in Germany, Hungary, Bulgaria, China – had not been encouraging. Worse still, the victories of Fascism in Italy and Nazism in Germany had shown that violently anti-communist movements could command mass support. The triumph of Franco in Spain was achieved in spite of the mobilization of international anti-Fascist forces and of appeals for a National Front, decimated behind the scenes by the direct manipulations of Soviet 'experts'. These set-backs restricted decisively the frontiers of communist operations outside the borders of the Soviet Union. The general staff of the International and the émigré communists in the Soviet Union felt the full fury of Stalin's Great Purge, and thousands of them perished. The activities of Comintern were placed under the surveillance of the organs of the Russian state. The Polish Party was dissolved. A similar fate nearly overcame the Yugoslavs. Others were reduced to terrified silence or became mere sounding boards of Stalinist slogans.

*This chapter was contributed by F. W. Deakin.

Comintern, once the symbolic headquarters of world revolution, shrank to a skeleton agency of the Soviet Party.

The outbreak of the Second World War in September 1939 seemed to revive in classic Marxist–Leninist terms the objective conditions of inevitable revolution following on the conflict of rival imperialisms. The neutrality of the Soviet Union was preserved by the Nazi–Soviet pact, guaranteeing in the short term the security of the Soviet Union and implying the early disintegration of the British and French empires. This act of Soviet statesmanship boldly disregarded the moral shock to the world communist movement and the consequent disarray of communist parties abroad. There were many defections: in France, for instance, twenty-four of seventy-eight communist deputies resigned from the party. But the blind loyalty of the old guard of 1919, and of those who had accepted every twist in Soviet policy for twenty years, would preserve a skeleton machinery in the face of desertions.

If Stalin's analysis was correct, the mobilization of the masses outside the Soviet Union would assume new forms under direct management. The phase of neutrality represented an ingenious tactical pause.

The collapse of France, the destruction of Czechoslovakia, the German military occupation of Norway, Denmark and the Low Countries was balanced in power terms by Soviet domination in Finland, by occupation of Eastern Poland and territories formerly part of the Czechoslovak and Roumanian states. The continued military resistance of Great Britain was unexpected.

All communist parties had received directives from Moscow to maintain strict neutrality in the 'imperialist' war and to undertake no action which might support the warring capitalist powers engaged in their mutual destruction.

In the early hours of 22 June 1941 the massive assault of the German armies along the Western frontiers of the Soviet Union revealed the extent of Soviet miscalculations. Russia was unexpectedly faced with a struggle for national survival.

Those Comintern officials who had survived the purges were evacuated over a thousand miles eastwards to the small town of Ufa in the Bashkir republic, while Dimitrov as Secretary-General and a group of senior foreign leaders were quartered (like the diplomatic corps) at Kuibyshev.

The whole organization was under the control of the Soviet

Foreign Ministry and its activities mainly confined to propaganda, and the setting up of radio stations such as 'Free Yugoslavia' to broadcast news to enemy-occupied Europe. These transmitters also sent enciphered messages from the leaders of national communist parties residing in Russia to such local leaders as had survived enemy police action in their several countries.

A school was also set up at Ufa to train national cadres for missions behind the battle fronts.

Since September 1939 Comintern as the voice of the Soviet government had instructed each local party in Europe to adopt an attitude of strict neutrality in the imperialist conflict. Collaboration with the war effort of Britain and Germany was denounced. Acts of resistance in countries occupied by the German armies, in Poland, Czechoslovakia, Norway, Belgium and Holland were discouraged. After the fall of France in June 1940, the French communist Politburo sought German permission to publish the Party press, and for a brief interlude deluded itself with the prospect of acting as a legal party.

Sabotage of the Vichy regime was encouraged by the hope of moving into the void of power created by the collapse of the French war government. The small band of Free Frenchmen under Colonel de Gaulle in London were denounced as 'lackeys of British capitalism'. If only the whole traditional political leadership of France, military and political, had fled the country at the moment of defeat – the French Communist Party leaders seem to have envisaged a National Front of all left elements controlled by themselves and functioning with German connivance in the spirit of the Nazi–Soviet pact.

The assault of the German armies on the Soviet Union in June 1941 shattered any such illusion, and, in any event, since September 1939 German police forces and collaborationist regimes, such as Quisling's in Norway, had proceeded to disrupt or drive underground the weakened cadres of local communist parties.

Without exception the communists of Europe had been absent from the early and spontaneous patriotic Resistance organizations which grew up from frail beginnings during the first two years of warfare on the Continent.

The Nazi attack on Russia enforced a total break with the immediate past, and an abrupt transformation in Soviet high policy. The Russian leadership now found itself not only with one major ally – Great Britain – but also in relations with the national governments and committees in exile from their countries and based on London. These bodies were officially recognized – with the exception of de Gaulle until 1943 – by the British government, as the future post-war representatives of liberated Europe in Poland, Norway, Holland, Belgium, Yugoslavia and Greece.

The Soviet Foreign Ministry, in the short-term political interest of the war-time alliance, decided within weeks of being at war to follow the example of Great Britain and to accord official recognition in each case to these exiled bodies.

Formal and public expression was also given by Moscow to the strategy of forming a broad patriotic National Front through the countries of enemy-occupied Europe. In so far as communications by radio or courier would permit, secret instructions to local communist leaderships were given in this sense, stressing the need to preserve Allied unity by avoiding the organization of independent and isolated communist resistance groups.

These directives were strengthened on the entry of the United States into the war in December 1941.

The slogan of National Unity in face of the threat of international Fascism was obediently taken up by all communist leaders. In Britain itself the Party conveyed the new message to the communists of India and the Commonwealth countries.

During the winter war of 1941 on the Eastern Front, and throughout the following year, the Soviet armies were on the defensive. Partisan units were organized in Soviet territories under German military occupation, on the model of 1919–20, but brought under the direct control of a special section of the Soviet High Command and confined to specific operations in a subordinate role.

This Soviet concept of irregular war was an established doctrine. Any future planning of resistance beyond the western frontiers of the Soviet Union was to be strictly co-ordinated with and governed by the progress of the Russian armies.

The prospect of spontaneous national communist revolutions taking premature control of any country before the final victory was viewed by the Russians with cautious hostility. They liked even less the idea of co-ordinated resistance movements supported by London and Washington in the name of exiled governments, in close contact with partisans operating within occupied Europe, and culminating in the return in each country of pro-Western regimes. But the dilemma was not immediate. The formal unity of the Grand Alliance must remain the first priority in the conduct of Soviet policy.

The Russians never adopted a theory of short-term patriotic resistance, grouping temporarily all national elements and limited to partisan action against enemy occupation. To them resistance was a minor and preliminary phase to be organized by party cells and action squads with a view to the ultimate mobilization of the masses to achieve complete social and political revolution. The early stages would be confined to establishing contact with the workers and peasants by highly trained groups of Party members, by spreading propaganda, by training for sabotage in the factories and on all lines of communications, and by recruiting at a given signal large bodies of militia from the populations of the cities to take over political power in the countryside on the eve of a communist D Day which would be marked by the appearance of the Soviet armies.

Whether or not resistance could lead to the revolutionary liberation of a particular country would depend on the strategic position of the Russian armies and those of their Western Allies at the moment of victory. The Russian attitude to European resistance was thus a direct reflection of the ultimate war aims of the Soviet Union.

The formal dilemma of Soviet policy during the first year of involvement in hostility with the Axis was first revealed in their attitude to events in Yugoslavia.

Here the small but highly organized Communist Party, reconstructed under Comintern instructions by Tito in 1937, and in radio and courier communication with Russia, called for an armed rising throughout the country according to plan and following on the appeal by telegram from Moscow in September 1941. From the beginning of the rebellion, negotiations punctuated by armed clashes were engaged with nationalist bands (chetniks) under Mihailović, but a rupture and a drawn out civil war parallel with spreading communist resistance against the Axis set a special and unique pattern. It marked the open rejection of any form of united National Front. The structure of Tito's Liberation Movement was utterly unlike that recommended by Moscow. The main striking force of the Yugoslav communist resistance was composed of

Proletarian brigades openly commanded by Party members and backed by political commissars. They had a dual role : immediate and continuous military action against the occupier in mobile warfare throughout the country, and the simultaneous creation of political authorities in each 'free territory' set up during the course of operations.

Within the first weeks of the rising the Yugoslav Party was bitterly criticized at meetings of the Balkan Secretariat of the Comintern for the premature launching of an irresponsible 'adventure' which would according to official doctrine isolate the peasant masses from the communists who would be speedily exterminated by the enemy.

The Soviet Foreign Ministry was also anxious to avoid complications with London where the Royal Yugoslav Government in exile – also formally recognized by Moscow – had appointed Mihailović as Minister of War. Up to July 1942 the Russians were reluctant to accept evidence presented by Tito of Chetnik collaboration with the Axis.

Tito's decision to set up a provisional administration in December 1942, again in defiance of Soviet policy, was regarded as a premature challenge to the Royal Yugoslav Government and an issue which should not have been raised until after the war.

But these differences of political tactics were deliberately blurred both by Tito and the Russians. The effective resistance movement now spreading throughout Yugoslavia under local communist leadership provided a focus for the whole region of south-eastern Europe, and Moscow sought, with some reservations, to exploit on a short-term basis the inevitable prestige accruing to Tito and to extend his leadership and example to those resistance groups forming in neighbouring Balkan countries.

Limited recognition by the British, early in 1943, of the military value of the Yugoslav National Liberation Movement helped to overcome Soviet hesitations. As the Soviet Union was not in a position to send material aid to the partisans within Yugoslavia it felt justified in experimenting with cautious encouragement of a Balkan communist federation under the leadership of Tito, who was an experienced and loyal official of the Comintern and closely associated with its Secretary-General, Dimitrov.

Already in September 1942 the Comintern had instructed Tito to send delegates to set up the central machinery of a Communist Party in Albania under Enver Hoxha and to train military units on the Yugoslav model. Communist Albania developed as a satellite of the Yugoslav Party until the end of hostilities.

On a more limited scale contacts were made with the Bulgarian Communist Party. A mission was parachuted to Tito with instructions from Moscow and infiltrated into Bulgaria. Small partisan units were formed within Yugoslav territory and sent to operate inside the country with modest results. Yugoslav delegates held joint talks with representatives of the underground Bulgarian Party.

Similar moves for a united Balkan Communist Front were made in Greece. Tito's special envoy, Svetozar Vukmanović-Tempo, paid several visits to the mountain headquarters of ELAS, the military formation of the Greek Communist Party. He found a confused situation. The communist bands were weak and led by regular officers. Their strategy was the conventional one – to destroy rival nationalist groups, to delay general military action against the occupier and to prepare for an eventual political revolution based on the cities at the end of the war. The Greek scene was further complicated by the presence of a well-organized and central British military mission whose direct control of operations was tacitly if reluctantly accepted by all resistance elements, including the communists.

A terse message from Tito to Tempo in mid-1943 ended any further development towards a Balkan federation under Yugoslav communist leadership. The reasons were soon apparent.

On 22 May 1943 the formal dissolution of Comintern was announced. The published statement of its Presidium offered no explanation of this dramatic decision. A further statement declared that thirty foreign communist parties had been consulted, presumably either through their representatives in Moscow or by radio links, and that they were in unanimous agreement. The official reasons were summarized by Stalin himself in an interview with Reuters. The abolition of the Communist International was designed to put an end to the lies that Moscow wished to interfere in the internal affairs of other countries, and that communist parties merely obeyed foreign instructions.

With the dissolution of the Comintern all patriots could now unite with progressive forces in their respective countries to create a common front of National Liberation. This would form the basis of a future international front against the menace of

Hitlerism and lay the foundations of the future co-operation of all nations on a basis of absolute equality.

This apparent revolution in Soviet policy was the result of a personal decision by Stalin. The ghost of World Revolution must be exorcised for the benefit of the Grand Alliance against Hitler. The image of the Soviet Union was to appear as that of a great patriotic nation possessing no hidden aims of international subversion.

The strategic initiative in the war had already passed out of Nazi hands. The military victory of Russia and the Western Allies was a matter of time, and its political implications must be considered and studied with cautious realism. A division of Europe was, in Stalin's mind, inevitable, and would be conditioned by the positions held by the armies of the victors at the moment of the end of hostilities.

At the last meeting of the Comintern Presidium there was some muted difference of opinion. The survivors of the old guard of 1919 gave way to sentimental lamentations and expressed doubts as to the future of proletarian internationalism. It was for the Italian leader, Togliatti, to stress the advantages for the post-war communist movement of the new idea of 'Polycentrism', the thesis of regional co-operation of communist parties finding themselves in a similar situation.

Although not expressed in explicit terms, the official abandonment of a central organization based on Moscow treating all local communist parties as national sections of such a body was received with general relief by the leaderships concerned, and for the reasons expressed by Stalin in his Reuter interview.

The French Communist Party had already escaped from the temporary isolation to which Moscow's directives after the Nazi–Soviet pact had condemned it. Two of the senior members of the Politburo, Thorez and Marty, had found their way to Moscow in the summer of 1940. At home the organization had adopted a kind of voluntary segregation preserving its cadres and underground 'central committee', and disseminating newspapers and brochures aimed at the Vichy regime as a permitted target, but avoiding attacks on the German occupation authorities.

The events of June 1941 prompted an immediate and calculated explosion of chauvinism appealing to the patriotic tradition of Valmy and the Jacobins. A National Front was proclaimed to appeal to all groups and classes. Starting with small cells of trusted Party members, the cadres of a future mass liberation movement were formed to infiltrate all structures and levels of French society. Early approaches to non-communist resistance groups which had formed since 1940 were rejected by the latter. But the possibilities of an independent and self-generated communist resistance of the interior in competition with the France Libre of de Gaulle supported, if cautiously, by British material aid, were non-existent. Directives from Moscow either by ciphered radio messages or through the Soviet Embassy which was maintained at Vichy almost certainly controlled tactical co-operation with de Gaulle, and the organizations which accepted his authority inside France. The mission of Jean Moulin to set up a unified Council of National Resistance succeeded in briefing the communist representatives, and delegates from the Party centre were sent to London and later to Algiers.

The military organization of the communist-controlled National Front formed under the label of Francs Tireurs et Partisans (FTP) – recalling the irregulars of 1870–1 – was nominally subordinate to the Gaullist military command. A façade of unity was thus constructed but it concealed widely different strategic concepts. The Gaullist leadership aimed at creating a regular Free French army based after 1943 on Africa, which would play an active role in the liberation of occupied France alongside the massive Anglo-American landings and harness to its military actions and political cause the resources of the Resistance of the Interior already organized for sabotage and intelligence by reliable agents sent from London or Algiers.

The FTP as the military arm of the National Front was not ambitious in structure and its command now lost sight of the ultimate goal of social revolution. The miseries of Vichy and German occupation had created by early 1944 massive and ill-defined popular support for a liberating movement.

The decision by the Vichy authorities under German pressure to conscript civilians for labour service in Germany led to the spontaneous flight of thousands of the young generation to the precarious refuges in the mountainous area of Western France, in the Vosges and the Alps of Savoy. The creation of local maquis took by surprise both the Gaullists and the communists. Both parties were in principle opposed to static strongholds held by ill-equipped and untrained groups lacking leaders and weapons. But the will to fight expressed by this sudden increase of potential manpower for action against the enemy had to be recognized. The roll of tragic heroes and martyrs steadily lengthened – the maquis of the Vercors and Glières, for instance, supplied from the air with instructors and inadequate arms were surrounded and destroyed by SS troops and Vichy militia.

The experiment was discouraged, but the problem of floating and disorganized groups of young Frenchmen remained, scattered through occupied France in flight from the towns and cities, where the offices of the STO (Service de Travail Obligatoire) were set up to conscript them.

The communists attempted with some success to retain small cadres in mountain areas near the main centres of population in groups of eight to ten men to help FTP parties on the move and to infiltrate back into the cities action squads for sabotage in the factories and to organize street fighting when the liberation began.

The Gaullists attempted to enrol others in units of the FFI (French Forces of the Interior) under their military command to which the FTP was in principle subordinated.

All parties were anxious to avoid a spontaneous and premature armed insurrection which could neither be equipped nor trained to fight the German army of occupation and would end in a national disaster. Resistance activity must it seemed be restricted to sabotage of communications, bursts of guerilla warfare against isolated German units and the collection of military intelligence for the advancing Allied columns. A national insurrection in France – the target of communist organization – played no part in Allied planning nor that of the Gaullist leadership in Algiers. The hopes placed by the French communist leaders in a rapid take over of the machinery of the Vichy administration, before the arrival of the Free French Forces together with the Anglo-American armies, and co-ordinated with mass insurrection in the main cities and ports backed by a mass mobilization of a people's militia, now materialized.

The FTP played their appointed role in due subordination to Allied directives with heroism and effect. Vital German reinforcements were delayed in their northward move to the battle front in Normandy. Active assistance was given to the Allied forces in the Southern landings in Provence.

The communist leadership was not prepared to face an open rupture with the Gaullist machinery of provisional administration during the critical days of the national liberation of France. The Algiers government of de Gaulle had already been recognized formally by Moscow as part of an overall political strategy in the interests of the Grand Alliance.

The Italian Communist Party had been the first victim of Fascism. Its organization had been disrupted and driven underground and the leadership either imprisoned or forced into exile during the years immediately following the March on Rome in 1922. Contact was maintained by occasional couriers between the party 'centre' established in Paris and the decimated cadres within Italy.

The exiled leaders in France were in intermittent touch with Moscow where the Italian communist group were recruited into the organization of Comintern. The Secretary General of the Italian Politburo, Palmiro Togliatti, managed to preserve a certain prestige for his party through his functions in the Secretariat of Comintern and as a travelling 'inspector'. He was put 'in charge' of the communist parties of Central Europe in the early 1930s and supervised the work of the Polish Party until its dissolution by Moscow. The role of Togliatti was further enhanced by his special mission to Spain in July 1937 as Comintern 'adviser' to the Spanish Communist Party, and later to establish control over the political work of the International Brigade, in which Italian communist exiles played a special part and were to form valuable cadres for their own future activities.

On the collapse of the Spanish Republic, Togliatti escaped to France and organized in Paris the 'centre' of the Italian Party. After arrest and imprisonment by the French authorities he was directed by underground channels to Moscow in the summer of 1940.

The arrival of Togliatti in Moscow had coincided with the entry of Fascist Italy into the war on the side of Germany. In view of Russia's neutrality, the Italian committee remaining underground in Paris and Togliatti and his group in Moscow were constrained to inactivity.

But in July 1941 one of the Comintern radio stations was put at his disposal and regular broadcasts to Italy were instituted. At the same time individual party organizers crossed the Franco–Italian border, and the work began of reconstructing the party cells in the northern cities, in Rome, Emilia and Tuscany. The party newspaper *Unitá* appeared on a clandestine press early in 1942. The first results of organization in the factories of the North appeared in the strikes of March 1943, which alarmed the Fascist authorities as a warning symptom. But the apparatus of the Fascist state was as yet unimpaired.

On the French pattern, a call for a National Front was disseminated and agreements reached in France with non-communist exiled groups, and tentative moves were made in the same direction by communist delegates in Italy towards the representatives of the pre-1922 parties.

The *coup d'état* of 25 July 1943 was carried out on the responsibility of the King by the Supreme Command, and those democratic elements stirring in isolated groups played no part in these events. The Badoglio government maintained the Fascist legislation banning the communists and rejected any inclusion of representatives of the former democratic parties.

The Italian communist group, however, preserved their new skeleton organization of cells intact and a directing party 'centre' which had been formed in Milan in July was reinforced by a similar underground committee in Rome.

The Italian armistice of 8 September 1943 and the flight of Badoglio and the King from Rome to seek Allied protection in Brindisi was followed by the setting up of the German-controlled puppet republic under Mussolini in the North at Salò on Lake Garda. Italy was within days split into two hostile camps cut by the battle front between the Allied and German armies. In both regions there was a void of power and potentially a revolutionary situation.

The embryonic National Front proclaimed among the exiled groups in France now assumed a firmer shape in the provisional Committee of National Liberation set up underground in Rome in September, and representing all anti-Fascist groups and the former democratic parties.

The communist leadership inside Italy was divided between the two centres in Milan and Rome. The leaders were faced with the issues which were henceforward to dominate their actions and attitude towards military assistance and its political forms. The Rome Committee of National Liberation, and even more aggressively its offshoot later established underground in Milan, were opposed to any collaboration with Badoglio and the Monarchy. Their members representing all shades of anti-Fascist politics,

145

including the communists, were agreed on a future Republic, though divided on its political structure. This basic stand was in open contrast to Anglo-American policy which recognized Badoglio as a co-belligerent government and implicitly accepted the continuity of the Italian Monarchy.

During September and November 1943 in the Alpine valleys of Piedmont and Lombardy small bands, led in most cases by regular army officers, formed the elements of armed resistance to the neo-Fascist enclave of Salò. Their formations were fluid and politically unorganized.

The Italian communist leadership was now faced with the dual problem of deciding on a firm course of military and political action which would not isolate the party from its allies in the Committee of National Liberation nor the spreading armed bands forming in the mountain regions north of the Appenine battle front.

The local leaders were inflexibly opposed to the Monarchy and to political dealings with Badoglio. The presence of resistance formations in the North in sympathy with the latter made necessary a compromise on the military level.

The communist 'centre' had begun long-term planning for armed insurrection based on the cities of North and Central Italy as early as May 1943. Action groups (GAP) were formed to attack collaborators and their German colleagues and to prepare industrial sabotage. After September special military units – the 'Garibaldini' – were formed in the hills and countryside and slowly a nominally unified command under the Committee of National Liberation in Milan was set up on similar lines as in France.

The danger of isolated and weakened politico-military action in Italy by unco-ordinated resistance elements out of touch and sympathy with the Anglo-Americans was however, greater than in France.

In October 1943 Togliatti broadcast from Moscow, insisting on tactical acceptance of the Badoglio regime to the dismay of the majority of the local communist leadership in Italy. On 13 March 1944 the Soviet government formally recognized Badoglio, and at the end of the month Togliatti travelled by devious routes to Naples.

His direct initiative imposed the formation of a government of national unity and its acceptance by the Communist Party.

The enforcement of wholesale conscription of the younger age groups into Mussolini's phantom army precipitated mass flights of men of military age to the hills in the North and in Emilia, Tuscany and Liguria – to the exclusive benefit of the partisan groups now increasingly organized under the control of the Committee of National Liberation. The communists were instructed to infiltrate into this extended structure of resistance. Togliatti used to the full his influence in the direction of unified political and military control.

The decision of the Grand Alliance at the Teheran conference in December 1943 to shift the strategic emphasis to the early launching of the Second Front in North Western Europe automatically reduced the Italian theatre to a secondary role. This action was directly connected with the marked lack of interest displayed by the Anglo-American Mediterranean Command in arming and directing Italian resistance north of the immediate battle front now pushed in slow exhausting stages northwards towards the Alpine frontiers of the Reich.

The dramatic secret armistice talks with the German military leaders in Northern Italy starting in January 1945 led to the local surrender of the German armies throughout this theatre in April.

The pace of events overtook any plan for a popular insurrection, and the role of the Italian resistance, armed reluctantly in limited quantities by the Western Allies, was confined to the temporary assumption of authority and the vital protection of industrial plants and port installations in the main cities of Northern Italy – a service of great importance but temporary in nature.

As in France, the Italian partisans performed valuable auxiliary functions and their political aims, varying according to internal Party loyalties, were fused into the general and uneasy climate of a new state recognized by the three partners in the Grand Alliance.

In the other countries of Northern and Western Europe which had endured Nazi occupation, in Norway, Holland and Belgium the role of the small local communist parties were marginal and confined to tactical action in strikes and occasional liquidation of collaborators and German officials. The firm institutional structures of these national governments as represented in exile in London precluded a programme of social revolution, and any such

147

action was sternly discouraged by Moscow. As Stalin put it characteristically in a message to Churchill and Roosevelt: 'And have I paid any attention to Belgium?'

The fate of resistance movements in Central and South Eastern Europe was inevitably bound up with long-term Soviet intentions in regard to future strategic security, the course of the last stages of the military defeat of Germany and the main western lines of advance of the Russian armies.

Stalin was calculatingly slow to reveal his hand. In October 1944 Churchill made the first diplomatic move, in informal fashion, to elicit at least a general hint. A small piece of paper was exchanged between the two leaders as an experimental and temporary expedient. It referred only to the Balkans, and implied a rough division of spheres of interest in the form of percentages: in Roumania 90 per cent Russian, in Greece 90 per cent British (in accord with the United States), in Yugoslavia and in Hungary 50–50, in Bulgaria 75 per cent Russian.

Although this scrap of paper has given rise to unstilled controversies Churchill was simply exploring the general intentions of Stalin's future policy in these regions. The Russians appeared not even to have kept a copy, but, in discussions on later developments in Roumania, and Greece, Stalin directly invoked this 'understanding'.

The main purpose of this meeting was to achieve a diplomatic solution at the summit of the political future of Poland, and this issue was to close in early tragedy.

In essence, but not in form, the Soviet government was pursuing a single aim: military occupation by the Russian armies of the German-occupied or controlled territories stretching from the Baltic to the Black Sea would be followed by the installation of political regimes friendly to the Soviet Union, varying according to local conditions from temporary coalition in a Russian-sponsored National Front to the early establishment of a communist-controlled administration.

Above all, the anti-Bolshevik sanitary cordon established in the form of a chain of new nation states under British and French influence after 1919 would be totally dismantled. In Central Europe, Poland and Czechoslovakia were regarded by Moscow as countries in which the Soviet Union had strategic interests no less vital than those of Britain in Greece. In the Balkans the Russians took a similar attitude in regard to Roumania and in a lesser degree to Bulgaria and Hungary.

They were content to regard it as a loyal satellite, and to accept his ultimate assumption of political power in Yugoslavia, while remaining suspicious of British support to the Yugoslav National Liberation Movement and unsympathetic to the independent military actions of a partisan army escaping direct Soviet control. But elsewhere, throughout these territories, there could be no compromises or concessions.

Conflict and controversy between the three partners in the Grand Alliance centred round the fate of Poland and were to extend to that of Czechslovakia. In both cases the British, and later the American, governments had undertaken precise diplomatic obligations. Britain had in addition taken on the responsibility for material aid to local resistance organizations in these countries on the same pattern as in France, Norway and the Low Countries. The purpose of this support was to facilitate at the end of hostilities the return of the Polish coalition government-in-exile to Warsaw, and of Beneš and his colleagues to Prague.

In anticipation of events, with British support limited by the demands of Britain's own war effort, a Polish Home Army (the AK) was formed after the German occupation in September 1939. A network of cadres was organized in face of massive German repression aimed at the destruction of the elite of the Polish nation. The early pattern of resistance in Poland was based on a patriotic and nationalist reaction to Nazi government. It excluded certain extreme right elements, and the remnants of the disbanded Polish Communist Party. It was not until January 1942 that the party was 'officially' reformed in the Soviet Union under Russian instructions, and the first attempts were made to parachute Soviet instructors to those small groups of local party members who had survived the events of 1939–41.

But Moscow had little faith in 'native' resistance organizations, and realized from the outset that in Poland there could be no question of building up a counter-government to the Home Army. Small partisan units could render limited services, and their symbolic existence must be established. But a general pattern of action was evolved by the Russians during the course of 1942 in regard to those countries which would lie in the path of the main Soviet advance. The Soviet armies would be accompanied by brigades or divisions formed out of national exiles or deserters from armies raised by satellite regimes under German influence.

Units such as the First Polish Division of General Berling would represent a symbolic national contribution to the military liberation of their countries.

Simultaneously, special party schools trained political cadres for the countries to be liberated. Their members were carefully selected from amongst communists formerly employed in the Comintern machine or in exile in Moscow. Their links with their countries of origin were tenuous, and communist groups at home were few and weak. The return of the exiles was totally dependent on Soviet support and control by specialist 'instructors'.

A Polish National Committee formed in Moscow in January 1944 was established by the Russians in Lublin in Eastern Poland in the following summer. The emergence of the elements of a communist counter-resistance, and military penetration in force from the East by the Russians, was the decisive reason for the precipitation by the Polish government in London, without formal consultation with the British, of the Warsaw rising directed by the command of the Home Army on 1 August 1944.

The tragic confusion which ensued is known in general outline and obscured in precise detail. The Soviet armies were on the opposite bank of the river Vistula and their advance was suddenly halted. Anglo-American attempts to send in adequate supplies by air proved to be technically unrealizable.

The rising of Warsaw was publicly disowned by the Russians, and the structure of the Home Army was liquidated.

Future Russian objectives in regard to Poland, in spite of intensive diplomatic moves by Britain and America to secure Soviet agreement on a unified Polish administration, proceeded according to plan.

In Czechoslovakia events took a less dramatic but similar course. Ever since the Munich agreement in 1938 President Beneš had regarded an understanding with Moscow as essential for the restoration and survival of the Czechoslovak state. After June 1941 he was more optimistic than any other political leader in exile from an occupied country about future relations with the Soviet Union.

In July 1941 the Russians recognized the Czechoslovak government in London and resumed diplomatic relations, which had been severed after the Nazi-Soviet pact. In December 1942 a formal treaty was signed by Beneš in Moscow. The Czechoslovak Council in London had already been broadened to include four communist representatives.

An underground Resistance Council had been set up inside the country at the time of Beneš' departure which did not include communists. The British attempted, as in the case of Poland, to support groups operating within former Czechoslovak territory and derived vital military intelligence regarding the Nazi war machine from these sources.

Embryo communist organizations appeared after the middle of 1942 based separately on the German Protectorate of Bohemia and the independent satellite state of Slovakia. During his visit to Moscow Beneš had discussions with Czechoslovak Communist leaders, and a working alliance with them was thenceforward a major objective of his policy, since the eventual liberation of his country would come from the East and by the advance of the Soviet Armies.

Soviet intentions with regard to the Czechoslovak state were not publicized, but their general direction was clear after 1943 when Czech units were formed in Russia separate from Slovak brigades built up from deserters from the army of the satellite state of Slovakia created by the Germans. The future Czecho-Slovakia was evidently seen as a loose federation in which strong Soviet influence was exercised through 'independent' Czech and Slovak Communist parties.

By the summer of 1944 the Soviet armies were close to the borders of Slovakia and the possibilities of an armed rising within the German satellite became abruptly apparent to the Russians and to Beneš and his advisers in London.

An underground Slovak National Council was set up which grouped nominally all anti-Fascist elements, and a military conspiracy developed within the 'official' Fascist Slovak army. Partisan groups were parachuted from the Soviet Ukraine into the mountain areas near the Eastern borders of the country to organize a parallel and competitive military resistance, but the national insurrection which exploded in August 1944 was essentially the work of units of the Slovak army.

The success of the rising could only be confirmed by the swift intervention of the Soviet armies. There were, however, sound military reasons why this did not take place and the Ukrainian Army Corps poised on the borders was unable to advance.

By November the rising was put down by the Germans with heavy loss of life. The lack of insurrectional experience on the part of the Slovak military leadership and lack of co-ordination with Soviet-organized partisan groups were matched on the political level by the incohesion of the Slovak National Council accepted in principle by both Beneš and the Russians.

The latter never again made a premature attempt to support a spontaneous national insurrection and the Slovak rising proved to be an isolated tragedy.

Scattered partisan groups survived in Slovakia until the final advance of the Red Armies in April 1945, and similar units and underground National Committees surfaced in Bohemia at the same moment. The liberation of Prague was a 'model' of symbolic armed insurrection in a large city, and was undisturbed by the proximity of the American forces advancing eastwards into Central Europe. As in the case of Poland, the final liberation of former Czech and Slovak territories was accomplished according to Russian planning.

In Bulgaria, Hungary and Roumania no effective indigenous resistance was conceived by Moscow nor could it form against regimes with long experience of anti-communist repression and in close alliance with the Axis. In Roumania and Bulgaria the final steps of liberation were decisively facilitated by the disciplined defection of their armed forces from the Nazi alliance, and their action as Soviet auxiliaries in the final campaign of the Russian armies against the Germans in the Hungarian plain and northwards through Slovakia and Bohemia to the Eastern frontiers of the Reich.

Local communist leaders trained in Moscow accompanied by 'symbolic' divisions in the case of Roumania, raised from deserters in the Soviet Union, arrived in the baggage train of the Russian armies to form the directing elements in the provisional anti-Fascist administrations set up as the first stage to an exclusively communist post-war take over of power.

The division of Europe into two political camps was completed in the confusion of the total victory of the Grand Alliance against the Third Reich.

18 Bologna, April 1945. Communist Partisans hand in their weapons

19 Berlin, May 1945. Soviet Army establishes authority that will, as everywhere else to the east in Europe, guarantee installation of Moscow-controlled democracies

20 Molotov signs Nazi-Soviet
non-aggression Pact, 1939

21 Comintern functionary Gottwal
in 1946 as Prime Minister in Czech
coalition government. By 1948, wit
help of KGB and 'action squads',
Communists able to seize full contr

22 British students show solidarity
with USSR in pre-war period of
diplomacy that led to Stalin-Hitler
Pact. Profound trauma wrought on
mass of left-wing sympathisers and
Communists alike

In Germany itself, the Soviet leadership experimented briefly with a Free German Committee uneasily composed of senior German generals captured on the Eastern Front and exiled survivors of the ill-fated German Communist party. But the savage lessons of the July plot in 1944 showed the impossibility of conspiratorial rising against Hitler, and the Russians improvised an alternative strategy. In those areas of Germany which would inevitably come under Soviet control a satellite regime headed solely by German communists, and aided by newly trained cadres of the younger generation formed in the Soviet Union, was to be established as a provisional government pending the settlement of the German problem at the conference table.

For communists the Second World War was a stage in the struggle with capitalism. After the German attack on the Soviet Union tactical collaboration with bourgeois democracy was necessary: but once Fascism was defeated the temporary allies would again be enemies. Communists, therefore, in their resistance to the Axis had an eye to the subsequent phase in the secular struggle.

As always, the Soviet Union was concerned with strengthening the conspiratorial revolutionary elite in urban centres and primarily amongst industrial workers. The activities of these cadres included sabotage, intelligence work and, most important of all, recruitment and training for a climactic urban-based uprising. Ideally, the uprising should be synchronized with the liberation of an occupied country by allied armies. It was more significant symbolically, and as a way of asserting communist political influence when the establishment of a new national government was in sight, than as a contribution to the defeat of the occupying power. As their criticisms of the Yugoslav communists in 1941 indicated the Soviet leadership had no use for the concept of total uprising while 'liberation' was still a remote prospect. Nor did they find it desirable that the peasantry should play a major role in resistance since this might create complications in the revolutionary stage of liberation. Partisan warfare was regarded as auxiliary to the military actions of conventional armies, and of limited significance.

This politically determined theory of resistance could not precisely govern the behaviour of communists. The desperate war made strange allies. In most occupied countries numerical weakness and police repression compelled communists to recruit support wherever they could find it, and to adopt whatever tactics were necessary to their survival. During the Warsaw Rising, for instance, Polish communists in the city fought side by side with the Home Army's units. Communist and non-communist resistance groups usually competed, and often clashed. Their fortunes would be determined in the end by the strategic balance between the members of the Grand Alliance. But in the meantime, mutual hostility did not always preclude co-operation against a more immediately menacing foe.

Only in Yugoslavia (and its client state Albania) did communist direction of resistance lead naturally to communist government after the war. Elsewhere in Eastern Europe weak communist parties were brought to power by the Soviet armies, – in Poland over the wreckage of a large and heroic non-communist resistance movement. In countries liberated by the Western allies the communists had no opportunity to determine the character of the post-war regime. In France and Italy, however, they participated briefly in coalition governments and became for the first time massive working class parties. Skilful recruiting and vigorous participation in the last stages of resistance to the Germans, and above all the popularity of the Soviet Union after its tremendous victories, helped the communists to win this position of influence. They retained it largely because they were automatically the major opposition parties in countries whose governments were committed to the Western alliance.

part 4
Postwar Communism

1

Stalin and the Cold War

If the imperialists should unleash a new war, said Stalin in 1939, many governments then ruling by the grace of God would be missing when it ended. The peoples would sweep away both the warmongering Fascists and the decadent semi-fascist or bourgeois democratic regimes which, out of greed or cowardice or hatred of the Soviet Union, had connived at or failed to oppose aggression. In the event no country did more than the Soviet Union to encourage Nazi aggression, nor shared so amply in its proceeds. An early stalemate in the West, leaving both Germany and the Soviet Union in possession of their gains, was Stalin's hope. Although subsequent Soviet writers have always claimed that the Nazi–Soviet pact was thought of only as offering a breathing space, it is clear enough that the German invasion took Stalin by surprise. The standard epithet attached to it – 'treacherous' – may be taken as a genuine expression of indignation against the breaker of a contract which Stalin for his part had every intention of honouring.

Ever since the German invasion, the Soviet Union has represented itself as the earliest, most consistent and indeed only whole-hearted opponent of Fascism, frequently hinting during the war and insistently claiming in retrospect that the Western allies dragged their feet in the struggle against Hitler and considered making a separate peace with him. Foreign communists, both those who had obediently followed Stalin in opposing the war of rival imperialisms (which meant in practice sabotaging the war effort of the Western democracies), and those whom the Molotov–Ribbentrop pact had outraged, eagerly accepted the story that Stalin's policy in the first two years of the war had been a tactical ploy, and they rallied to the Soviet Union in its new role.

The Soviet Union sustained the main onslaught of the German land forces and shattered them. Soviet losses, human and material, were much heavier than those of other members of the anti-Hitler

157

coalition. As a result of these victories and these sacrifices Russia's international standing was higher in 1945 than at any time since the defeat of Napoleon. Admiration and gratitude to the Soviet armies and people swelled the ranks of the communist parties in some liberated countries – notably France and Italy – and created a fund of goodwill towards the Soviet Union in Western Europe and the United States. The Western allies accepted that the post-war settlement must take into account the security interests of the Soviet Union: in particular, they recognized a legitimate Soviet interest in the complexion and policies of the post-war regimes in Eastern and Central Europe, and agreed to a joint administration of Germany and Austria. As a result of the war, the Soviet borders were extended by the incorporation of territories (nearly all of them former provinces of the Tsarist Empire) 682,809 square kilometres in area, and with a population (in 1939) of almost 23 millions. The Western allies agreed, expressly or tactitly, to these Soviet acquisitions, though not without misgivings in the case of the three Baltic states occupied by the Red Army in 1940 and formally incorporated after fraudulent elections. But the expansion of the Soviet empire was not limited by the re-drawn frontiers. On the Soviet periphery, as inside the Soviet Union itself security, for Stalin, implied total control. In one after another of the countries liberated and temporarily occupied by the Soviet armies he installed governments first dominated by and subsequently in most cases solely composed of communists. These changes were presented as an expression of the people's will: the masses had as Stalin had foretold, renounced their old reactionary and anti-socialist rulers and enthusiastically embraced 'popular democracy' and eternal friendship with the Soviet Union. The cynicism of this claim was especially blatant in the case of Hungary and Roumania, where the ruling parties were in 1945 tiny exotic imports, or Poland, where fierce anti-Russian sentiments and dislike of Communism were endemic. Communists in these countries could not have established themselves in power without the Soviet military presence. In Bulgaria the traditional Russophilia of the common people might have allowed the communists in any case to play a major role, but the issue was not left to chance: there as elsewhere, rigged elections held under the auspices of the Soviet occupation forces delivered the country over to them. In Czechoslovakia, where the communists had commanded some genuine working class support between the wars, a mixed government including communists, subservient in its foreign policy to Soviet wishes but fully autonomous in internal affairs, ruled for two and a half years. Strains within the coalition, aggravated by Soviet pressures, wrecked it, and the communist coup in February 1948 brought the country into the ranks of the 'people's democracies'.

In Yugoslavia the communists had won great popularity at home and the respect of the Western allies by their leadership of the most heroic and effective of all partisan movements. On territory held by the partisans they had built the framework of a national administration. Though they acknowledged that allied victories over the Germans, and particularly the Soviet sweep into South Eastern Europe, created the conditions for their own final victory they none the less held that Yugoslav soil had been cleared of invaders mainly by Yugoslav efforts. They had no need of Soviet help to assume power. Indeed, it would have needed a massive military intervention to dislodge a broadly based and firmly united government with no cohesive political rival in sight, and with large disciplined and enthusiastic military forces at its disposal. It seemed likely that the Yugoslavs would play within the international communist movement a part second only to that of the Soviet Union itself.

In the Far East, the Soviet Union's eight-day war against Japan made possible the establishment of a communist regime under Soviet protection in North Korea, and the transfer to the Chinese People's Army of captured Japanese arms and equipment in large quantities. Stalin however does not seem to have thought that a communist conquest of all China was imminent. He accepted Chiang Kai Shek's status as a member of the 'Big Five', treated the Kuomintang government with unfailing diplomatic correctness, and urged tactical co-operation with their rivals on the Chinese communists. Elsewhere in Asia, communists were numerous only in Indonesia, where for the time being however, like the nationalists, they were precariously united by hostility to the Dutch. Among nationalists and Communists alike there were some who had resisted the Japanese, and others who had collaborated. Both political movements were rent by the personal rivalries of leaders eager to dominate the post-colonial regime.

In Europe outside the Soviet military sphere strong communist parties had emerged in France and Italy, powered by a general revulsion against the pre-war and war-time regimes, by widespread admiration for the feats of Soviet arms, by patriotic pride in the story of national resistance in which the communist role grew steadily with the telling, and by the militancy of workers faced with demands for hard and hungry work to repair a war-ravaged economy. In both countries, and in Belgium, communists held office in post-war coalition governments. It is doubtful whether Stalin expected in the short run more from his Western followers than a moderating influence on the foreign policies of their governments. A communist attempt to seize power in Italy or France (by means for instance of a general strike, and perhaps using weapons stockpiled by resistance units) would have dangerously exacerbated Britain and the United States, and if successful would have created communist governments separated from the Soviet military sphere by British and American forces, and so out of Soviet control. Stalin's view of the matter may be inferred from his remark to a Yugoslav leader that the French and Italian communists had not won power because 'we were unable to come to their aid'. President Roosevelt had assured Stalin that when the war ended American forces would be withdrawn from Europe within two years. If his successor had carried out this intention a communist attempt to seize power in France and Italy at that stage would have been a likely result. As it was, the communists temporarily strove to show themselves loyal and co-operative partners in coalition governments, though in France for instance this entailed amongst other things a refusal to encourage disruptive strikes, and an ambiguous attitude to the Algerian independence movement, which placed a great strain on party loyalties. It became impossible for Communists to remain in Western European governments which accepted American aid under the Marshall plan. Their departure, in the autumn of 1947, aroused fears of prolonged political crisis and serious industrial disorders, which proved to be exaggerated.

The breakdown of co-operation between communists and bourgeois parties in France, Italy and Belgium was a somewhat belated reflection at the local level of the breakdown in international co-operation between the Soviet Union and its war-time allies. The war had brought two military giants into being: the Soviet Union and – stronger of the two – the United States. Jointly, they could have dominated and determined the future of the rest of the world. Singly, either of them could have dominated most of Europe and Asia if the other had withdrawn into isolation. It is conceivable that these two super-powers would have found harmonious co-operation impossible even if they had been ideologically closer, and more nearly equal in economic strength. As it was, Stalin had always assumed that war-time collaboration only postponed an inevitable clash of interests. As he saw it the enormous expansion of American military and economic strength, and the spread of American influence, in themselves threatened the Soviet Union. Co-operation with the United States from a position of relative weakness would mean in effect submission to American dictates. Stalin's objectives therefore were to achieve parity with the United States in military and industrial strength as quickly as possible; in the meantime, to improve the Soviet Union's strategic position by territorial expansion wherever this was possible without risk of war; to exclude American influence from areas under his control, whatever the wishes of their inhabitants; and to undermine the 'positions of imperialism' (i.e. of the United States and its allies) through communist-led liberation movements in colonial or ex-colonial countries, and through Communist parties and front organizations in the capitalist countries themselves.

Stalin's domestic policies quickly made plain his view that peace meant no more than a continuation of the struggle against capitalism on other fronts and by other means. The precautionary imprisonment of Soviet soldiers released from prisoner of war camps and civilians returning from forced labour, the extirpation of 'cosmoplitan' and 'bourgeois' influences which had crept into the arts and the world of entertainment during the war, the ruthless purge of unreliable elements (including many communists) in annexed territories, the proclamation of a new heavy industrial programme demanding heavy sacrifices in order to 'guarantee us against all eventualities', dispelled all hope in the Soviet Union of a more comfortable, more relaxed and less xenophobic life.

The programme of strategic expansion was carried out skilfully, without concern for the susceptibilities of the Western democracies, but with a careful calculation of risks. In the case of Poland, Hungary, Roumania, Bulgaria and later Czechoslovakia the West could only register protests against the installation of unrepresentative and dictatorial satellite regimes. Where the risk of a direct military clash was greater Stalin was more cautious.

161

F*

The Greek communists, for instance, who controlled one of the more active resistance groups in that country, carried on guerilla warfare until 1949, with much assistance to begin with from their communist neighbours to the north, but with no hope of anything more than moral encouragement from the Soviet Union once the proclamation of the Truman doctrine in 1946 had brought Greece and Turkey under the American umbrella. Similarly, the Soviet Union after prolonging its occupation of Northern Iran for some six months beyond the agreed date, in the hope of establishing a pro-Soviet regime in 'Southern Azerbaijan' if not throughout Iran, yielded at last to Western pressure, withdrew and allowed its client government to collapse. Tension between East and West reached its highest point in 1948. Even the pretence of joint allied administration of Germany had by now broken down. The Soviet Union and the Western powers were at odds both over the problem of reunification, and over immediate economic policy: whereas the West was heavily subsidizing German economic reconstruction the Soviet Union was intent on bleeding Germany to accelerate its own recovery. In the summer of 1948 the Soviet Union blockaded Berlin, in the hope of eliminating the Western presence and assimilating the old capital into its own zone. For some weeks war seemed close: but the Soviet Union refrained from using its own planes to frustrate the air lift operation by which the West supplied Berlin with food and fuel, and finally abandoned the blockade. On one occasion only the Soviet Union seemed to have dangerously miscalculated. This was in 1950, when the communist government of North Korea launched an attack against the South, emboldened no doubt by American statements which seemed to renounce any continuing interest in Korea. In the war which followed the United States and its allies, fighting under the flag of the United Nations, carefully restricted their operations to the Korean peninsula, and the Soviet Union, though it sent supplies and experts to the North and mounted a tremendous propaganda campaign against the United States, committed no forces of its own to battle. None the less, the intervention of the infant communist regime in China for a time carried with it the danger of an extension of American operations beyond the Yalu River, and the involvement of the Soviet Union alongside China in a general Far Eastern war.

A vast and mostly superfluous literature has grown up on the origins and development of the cold war. There is of course room

for differences of opinion on the wisdom and morality of particular
initiatives and responses in the policies of all the countries involved. But on one point there can be no argument: Stalin in his
own elaborations of Leninist theory, and particularly in his frequent restatements of the lessons of 'Imperialism – the Highest
Stage of Capitalism', made plain his view that peaceful co-
existence between 'capitalism' and 'socialism' was possible only for
a limited period, and lasting peace attainable only through the
final triumph of 'socialism' after a 'series of frightful clashes'. It
was, therefore, entirely logical that he should, soon after 1945,
proclaim the division of the world into two irreconcilable camps,
led by the Soviet Union and the United States, that he should set
the 'camp of socialism' the task of making itself invulnerable and
impenetrable to capitalist encroachments, and that in the meantime he should refuse any international co-operation in which the
Soviet Union would necessarily appear as a junior partner. Thus,
the Baruch plan for the control of atomic weapons was unacceptable simply because it would cut across Soviet development of
those weapons, and the prospect of eventual military superiority
which this offered. And similarly, he not only rejected American
aid under the Marshall Plan on behalf of the Soviet Union, but
forbade Finland and Czechoslovakia (not yet communist) to take
advantage of it, since acceptance, as he saw it, must mean an
increase of American influence and American interference in the
area concerned.

The doctrine of the two camps was solemnly proclaimed by
Andrei Zhdanov in September 1947 when representatives of the
Albanian, Bulgarian, Czechoslovakian, Hungarian, Polish,
Roumanian, Soviet, Yugoslav, French and Italian Communist
parties met in Poland to found a new international communist
organization. This body, as its limited membership and its name
(Communist Information Bureau–Cominform) indicated, had a
more modest function than that which Comintern had nominally
discharged – the co-ordination of the world communist movement. The policy of each particular communist party, including
those of Eastern Europe, remained as it had long been a matter for
direct and secret discussion with the Soviet Union. Cominform's
ostensible function was the exchange of information on matters of
common concern, and even this in practice meant no more than
the issuing of joint statements, usually in terms already familiar
from the Soviet press, and the publication in various languages of

a newspaper called 'For a Lasting Peace and a People's Democracy', and of other propaganda material. Since the Soviet Union could obviously always command a majority within Cominform, Stalin may also originally have intended to use it as a means of applying additional pressure to any member whose performance fell short of his requirements. Thus, at the foundation meeting the French and Italians found themselves 'in the dock', accused of a lack of militancy in the crisis created by the Marshall Plan offer. Their main critics were the Yugoslav representatives, briefly enjoying their Party's role as the major communist party in power apart from the Soviet Party.

As it turned out, the most if not the only important subsequent meeting of Cominform was that held in June 1948 to expel the Yugoslav Communist Party. They were charged, amongst other things, with nationalism, the suppression of democracy within the Party, an attempt to liquidate the Party itself, and a highhanded and unfriendly attitude to the Soviet Union which ill became those who owed their freedom to the Soviet armed forces. Vague as these menacing complaints were they pointed to the real origins of the quarrel, which were later fully revealed by the Yugoslavs themselves. Tito and most of his senior colleagues had stoutly and indignantly resisted what they regarded as Soviet encroachments on their independence: excessive interference and the planting of Soviet agents in governmental agencies, intrigues intended to build up a group in the party whose first loyalty would be not to Tito but to Stalin. From its side, the Soviet Union perhaps had reason to suspect the Yugoslavs of aspiring to a regional hegemony in the Balkans. In any case, there was no place in Stalin's scheme for any but unquestioningly docile communist parties. He believed that his fulminations would bring down Tito without losing Yugoslavia: 'I will wag my little finger and he will disappear'. But Tito's strength lay in his position as a nationalist leader, and neither the rank and file of the Party (recruited for the most part during and after the war, and led by old partisans) nor the people at large were dismayed by Stalin's displeasure. The Cominform resolution urged Yugoslav communists to put 'true internationalists' in the place of their present leaders. Tito in fact had already decapitated the pro-Soviet minority within the Party by imprisoning two Central Committee members, Hebrang and Zujović. Some compromised diplomats and senior officers, including the Chief of Staff, fled the country, but the Party and government at large stood solidly behind Tito. The Soviet bloc broke off trade relations with Yugoslavia, savagely abused Tito as a Trotskyite, a fascist and an American stooge, and called repeatedly for his overthrow. At first, Tito sought to rebut the accusations against him by showing himself more Stalinist than Stalin, by accelerating the assimilation of Yugoslavia to the Soviet model. But he was saved by his flexibility: without prejudice to his independence in international affairs he entered into defence pacts with his non-communist neighbours, and obtained economic aid and arms from the United States. Similarly, he abandoned the Soviet model and from 1950 onwards encouraged the elaboration of a specifically Yugoslav socialism, with 'workers' self-management' as its most distinctive institution.

The Soviet–Yugoslav quarrel disturbed and embarrassed many Communist parties outside the Soviet bloc. None the less, there were few defections. Whatever their secret misgivings, most communist leaders dutifully anathematized Tito, and, worse still, pretended to take at their face value the accusations shortly brought against a number of highly placed communists in satellite countries. Tito's crime was to resist the tighter control which Stalin was determined to impose throughout his empire. The shakier communist regimes of East and Central Europe could not resist. They accepted, willy-nilly, the implanting of Soviet advisers in key positions, particularly in the defence ministries and the security services. They accepted the replacement by Soviet nominees of high government and party officials who had incurred Soviet displeasure, or (as was the case of several leading Czechoslovak Communists who had returned from emigration in the West) were simply not well known in Moscow. When Stalin decided to brace the East European parties by bloodletting he met with an enthusiastic response only in Hungary and Bulgaria. Rakosi and Chervenkov, First Secretaries of the Hungarian and Bulgarian parties respectively, and both former high Comintern officials, seized the opportunity to rid themselves of more attractive rivals by judicial murder. Laszlo Rajk, the Hungarian Minister of the Interior, and Traicho Kostov, the Bulgarian Deputy Prime Minister, were tried and executed as traitors and agents of foreign intelligence services. Besides their co-defendants thousands of others followed them into oblivion. Hundreds of thousands were expelled from the larger East European Communist parties (the Polish, Czechoslovak and East German) in the course of a characteristically Stalinist campaign to reinforce discipline by prophylactic terror. In one after another of the satellites groups suspected of nationalist deviation were stripped of office, though the reality behind the charges against such leaders as Gomulka in Poland was simply their attempt to create an illusion that their meticulously orthodox policies were spontaneously generated by local needs and not dictated from Moscow. For whatever reasons, the 'healthy' Polish leadership under Bierut, although they dutifully arrested their disgraced colleagues, deliberately delayed any further proceedings against them, and were in the end delivered by Stalin's death from the need to prove their loyalty by complicity in murder. Gottwald and the Czechoslovak leaders were equally reluctant to destroy old comrades, but their resistance collapsed when the Soviet secret police established its own all-powerful enclave within the Czechoslovak security services, built up an elaborate and totally fictitious case against a number of high functionaries and threatened to number anyone who sought to protect them, including if necessary Gottwald himself, amongst their accomplices. In November 1951 Slansky, former Secretary of the Central Committee, and Clementis, former Foreign Minister, were the main defendants in a show trial more startlingly grotesque than its predecessors, both because the standard indictment for treason was enriched with a new charge as ominous in its implications as it was absurd – that of collusion with international Zionism – and because this barbaric Stalinist ritual was for the first time enacted in a country with a tradition, only recently suppressed, of democracy, political tolerance and independent courts.

Stalin's successes in the post-war period were domestic. Savage discipline and an investment policy which cruelly pinched the consumer carried the Soviet Union into second place among industrialized countries. The balance sheet of his foreign policy was unimpressive. Yugoslavia was alienated. Communist hopes were defeated in one country after another: Greece, Iran, Malaya, Korea. The numerically strong parties in Italy and France were hampered by their role as Soviet auxiliaries. The French Party had remarkably little impact on the policies of the Fourth Republic towards Algeria and Indo-China. Such ambitious enterprises as the World Peace Campaign, with its massive demonstrations and its petitions signed by millions, had no visible influence on Western governments. The activities of the World Council for

Peace were indeed well symbolized by Picasso's featureless and obviously dyspnoeic dove. The official Soviet view was and is that only Soviet might, reinforced by the growing support of the peace-loving masses everywhere, deterred the American war-mongers, verbally and visually identified in Soviet propaganda as direct successors of the Nazis, from a thermo-nuclear assault on the Soviet Union. But this, like his morbid obsession with sub-version inside the 'socialist camp', was the fantasy of a senile dictator out of touch with reality.

The one major gain for the world communist movement be-tween 1945 and 1953 was apparently not altogether expected by Stalin nor unreservedly welcome. This was the communist con-quest of all mainland China, and the establishment of the Chinese People's Republic in 1949. The Soviet press was of course unstint-ing in its paeans and insistent on the contribution of Soviet aid to this 'greatest event since the October Revolution'. In December 1949 Mao Tse-tung led a powerful Chinese delegation to the celebrations of Stalin's seventieth birthday in Moscow, and after weeks of hard bargaining the two countries concluded a Treaty of Alliance, together with territorial and economic agreements. Mao appeared to have accepted a junior partnership with the Soviet Union. But his group in the past had often found it necessary to defy or tacitly ignore Comintern and Soviet advice. Mao had an ominous record as an ideological improvizer, and unlike Stalin did not trouble to camouflage his innovations: 'Russian Marxism' and 'Stalinism' were terms used only by anti-Soviet writers, but 'Maoism' and 'the Sinification of Marxism' were respectable con-cepts in China. When he was within sight of power Mao had recognized that an accommodation with the United States might be essential to the survival of his regime. The Sino-Soviet agree-ment of February 1950, which left Port Arthur, Dairen and the Manchurian Railway temporarily under Soviet control, was no doubt accepted by both sides as a strategic necessity until the new Chinese People's Republic was safe against American inter-vention. But from Stalin's point of view it also offered safeguards against an excessively independent Chinese foreign policy.

2

Stalin's Successors, the Thaw and the Collapse of Communist Internationalism

When Stalin died in March 1953 the need for more flexibility in home and foreign policy had long been evident, and indeed there were signs that he himself contemplated initiatives to win more room for manoeuvre in relations with the West, and to rescue Soviet agriculture from its prolonged and dangerous stagnation. It was perhaps as a prelude to startling changes of policy that he also began preparations for a major purge which threatened some of his closest colleagues. The execution of a Politburo member, A. Voznesensky, in 1949 (unannounced at the time), and the public denunciation in January 1953 of a 'doctors' plot' to assassinate a number of prominent persons, suggested that Stalin was reverting to the methods which he had used in the thirties to put his authority beyond challenge.

The news of his death was accompanied by warnings from his senior lieutenants against the dangers of 'disarray'. They had in mind not least the dangers of an open power struggle within the Soviet establishment, for Stalin had carefully balanced his colleagues against each other, and allowed no one to build a secure and autonomous base of personal power. The one apparent exception was Beria, head of the secret police: and the other senior party leaders quickly combined, in alliance with some of the generals, to remove and execute him, reduce the activities of the police, and bring them firmly under collective Party control. Their resolve to prevent the emergence of a second Stalin showed itself also in the separation of the two key posts which he had held: Malenkov held office as President of the Council of Ministers until February 1955, while Khrushchev was senior secretary of the Central Committee from March 1953, and was formally elected First Secretary in September of that year.

In curbing the police and forming a 'collective leadership' Stalin's successors were no doubt concerned for their own skins. But they also saw that Stalin's crude methods, effective enough in the 'second revolution' of the early thirties, during the war, and in the first years of post-war reconstruction, had become damaging and dangerous. They set themselves three main tasks: to reduce tension between the two camps and exploit opportunities for diplomatic gains which Stalin had neglected; to correct alarming imbalances in the Soviet economy; and to improve relations between the regime and the hard-pressed, cowed and resentful Soviet population. There were differences within the leadership as to the peace and scope of change, but not as to its direction.

In foreign policy the new regime hastened to join with the Western powers in liquidating the Korean war and pacifying Indo-China. After the successful negotiations on this subject in April–June 1954 the 'spirit of Geneva' became a stock phrase to describe the new atmosphere which Stalin's successors had created in international relations. Unlike him, they were ever ready to travel, to negotiate, to trade concessions. And there could be no mistaking their passionate concern to avoid war. When Malenkov said that thermo-nuclear conflict would mean the end of civilization he was surely speaking for his colleagues, although Khrushchev could not resist the retort that it would only mean the end of capitalism.

Stalin had reacted slowly to the beginnings of decolonialization, and looked suspiciously on governments created by the peaceful transference of power. Nehru, for instance, he saw as a post-colonial caretaker for the interests of imperialism. His successors quickly abandoned this position. In November–December 1955 Khrushchev, together with Bulganin (who had succeeded Malenkov in May), made a spectacular tour of India and Burma. In September 1955 the Soviet Union offered military aid to the regime of Colonel Nasser in Egypt, overlooking his suppression of the Egyptian Communists. The Soviet commitment to India and to Egypt would grow steadily in the next two decades, as the Soviet Union asserted more and more boldly its strategic interest in South Asia and the Eastern Mediterranean.

At home, the new Soviet regime quietly dissolved the atrocious labour camps, rehabilitated (often posthumously) thousands of innocent persons, condemned all infringements of 'socialist legality'. Theoretical discussions of the role of the individual in history, increasingly infrequent and restrained public references to Stalin, and constant hints that the leadership was engaged in restoring 'Leninist' norms, were meant as assurances of a break with the Stalinist past. More direct criticisms of the corrupt petty tyrants who had flourished under Stalin began to appear in plays and in novels. One of these, Ehrenburg's *The Thaw*, gave a name to the whole complex phenomenon of cautious reform. The Soviet population at large found more concrete earnest of the regime's goodwill in its programmes to increase the output of consumer goods and improve the food supply.

In the satellite countries Stalin's death had stirred longings for greater independence, a relaxation of harsh discipline, and higher living standards, which found immediate expression in riots in East Berlin and in Pilsen. These were quickly suppressed. The Soviet leaders left the satellite regional dictators to find their own formula for relaxation. But they had none of the advantages of a successor regime: they were themselves little Stalins, with their own personal cults, and personally answerable in the eyes of their peoples for the 'errors' of the Stalin period. An attempt in Hungary to improve the image of the regime by giving Imre Nagy responsibility for the 'new course', without taking the Party out of Rakosi's hands, was shortly abandoned. Obsolete leaders remained in place, while in some Eastern European countries expectations of reform grew clamorous.

The explosion of 1956 in Eastern Europe was set off by two events. In December 1955 Khrushchev and Bulganin visited Belgrade, where they apologized publicly for Stalin's treatment of Yugoslavia, feebly putting the blame on Beria (who of course had been 'unmasked' as an agent of imperialism). In seeking not merely a rapprochement between governments (which was quite sufficient in the eyes of the cautious Molotov) but the restoration of Party ties, Khrushchev had legitimized the specific form of socialism devised by Yugoslavia for its own needs, and quite distinct from the Soviet model. The effect of this in other East European countries was to weaken Soviet ideological authority, excite interest in possible local variants of 'national communism' with Yugoslavia as a promising exemplar, and revive the memories of communists destroyed or dismissed by those now in power as national deviationists or Titoists. In the following months Yugoslav criticism of the more hidebound East European regimes and particularly of Rakosi, aggravated discontent.

The second event which helped to precipitate open rebellion in Eastern Europe was the Twentieth Congress of the CPSU in February 1956, or more specifically Khrushchev's 'secret speech' denouncing Stalin. Its contents were quickly disseminated through the Party network, and leaked into the foreign press. Part of Khrushchev's intention was to reinforce his own supremacy and to equip himself with weapons against other leaders – especially Molotov and Malenkov – who had, he would later suggest, been deeply implicated in Stalin's crimes. But his Leninist revivalism, his determination to recharge the Soviet population with enthusiasm for the purposes of the regime, his intolerance of bureaucratic inertia all impelled him to dramatize his break with the past. In the Soviet Union itself the Twentieth Congress generated exaggerated hopes of a new deal. In the autumn there were reports of serious indiscipline provoked by 'rotten elements' in Soviet universities, and of sporadic strikes. But the impact of the speech was far more serious in Poland and in Hungary.

In June the workers of Poznan went on strike while an International Trade Fair was in progress, and were suppressed by force. Soviet publicity, as always, blamed subversive agents of the West, but the Polish leaders more wisely took legitimate grievances into account. In the course of the summer mass meetings and demonstrations demanding reform, and encouraged by dissident intellectuals whose most effective medium was the student newspaper *Po Prostu*, took place in Warsaw and other cities. Within the Polish leadership there was a struggle between the Stalinist Natolin group and the supporters of Gomulka, who had been expelled as a national communist in 1949, released from gaol in 1954, but not rehabilitated. This faction was strengthened by the previous dismissal of Stalinists from high positions in the security forces, and the tactful removal of the Soviet Marshal Rokossovsky from the Politburo in September. When the Central Committee convened on 19 October there were wild public demonstrations in favour of Gomulka. Khrushchev, with a Soviet delegation so composed as to show that there were no divisions on this subject in the Soviet Presidium, flew in to prevent the election of Gomulka as First Secretary. It was made clear to him that, short of military intervention which Polish troops would resist, he was helpless. Reluctantly he accepted Gomulka's pledges of loyalty, which included a promise not to demand the withdrawal of Soviet troops.

In the meantime, a revolutionary situation had developed in Hungary. The removal of Rakosi in July, and the rehabilitation and ceremonial re-interment of Rajk, had encouraged demands for greater freedom and measures of economic relief. The 'Polish October' was greeted with mass meetings and street demonstrations in Hungary. When the security police opened fire on demonstrators on 23 October, revolutionary committees sprang up all over the country, and Hungarian troops refused to move against the rebels. The temporizing government of Ernö Gerö collapsed, and Imre Nagy was swept to power. The triumphant masses celebrated their victory with a massacre of AVH (security police) agents. Nagy felt unable to stabilize the situation without help from other political forces, and formed a coalition government. He also sought the withdrawal of Soviet troops, and the recognition of Hungary's neutrality. These simultaneous threats to one-party rule, and to their military control of Central Europe, were too much for the Soviet leaders. On 4 November Soviet armoured forces invaded. Fighting went on for several days, and nearly 200,000 Hungarians fled across the unguarded frontiers, while the Soviet armies imposed a reliable client regime under Janos Kadar on a bleeding and prostrate country.

The bloody repression of a popular uprising greatly weakened the moral authority of the CPSU in the communist world. The Chinese, and more openly the Yugoslavs, were critical of Moscow's heavy-handed bungling, though they accepted the need for military intervention once Nagy had been carried away by the forces of counter-revolution. In the West thousands of disillusioned intellectuals, many of whom had observed Stalin's atrocities without a demurring whisper, now left the communist parties. More serious, from the Soviet point of view, was the increasing wariness and detachment of the communist leadership in some countries, notably Italy.

At the Twentieth Congress Khrushchev had made certain ideological pronouncements which, though less novel than was generally supposed, had important implications for the future of Soviet foreign policy, and the role assigned by it to foreign communist parties. He denied, to begin with, that war was 'fatally inevitable'. This was generally taken as a renunciation of Stalin's (and Lenin's) view that armed struggle between socialism and capitalism could be postponed by tactical 'co-existence', but not indefinitely. Khrushchev's amendment was long overdue, in the age of thermo-nuclear weapons. Stalin, in 1952, had offered only a hollow assurance that the next major conflict might be between rival capitalist powers. His Soviet audience must have remembered that this was his description of the Second World War until the Soviet Union itself was attacked.

Khrushchev's second seminal declaration was that Communist parties in capitalist countries might come to power by the parliamentary road. Subsequent glosses acknowledged that the proletariat might still have to use force against the recalcitrant bourgeoisie. The examples given of socialist regimes established by peaceful parliamentary means were those of the Baltic States (incorporated in the Soviet Union on popular demand organized by occupying Soviet armies) and Czechoslovakia (where a communist government brought to power by a parliamentary crisis had, under Soviet protection, abrogated the constitution and abolished free elections). None the less. Khrushchev's two complementary statements were widely understood as a proclamation that war with the West, and the promotion of revolution in capitalist countries, were no longer serviceable instruments of Soviet policy.

Khrushchev's own vision of the future was unfolded after he had defeated in June 1957 a powerful coalition of rivals – the 'anti-Party group', which was later revealed to have included a majority of his colleagues in the Presidium of the Central Committee. He envisaged the triumph of socialism over capitalism in 'peaceful economic competition'. The Soviet Union, already (according to Khrushchev) well on the way to overtaking the United States, would increasingly assert its economic strength, in ways left somewhat vague, to weaken the positions of imperialism. A prosperous, and socially harmonious, Soviet Union would be irresistibly attractive to the peoples of capitalist states, while underdeveloped countries would hasten to adopt the Soviet model, and to ally themselves with the socialist camp in the anti-imperialist struggle.

Khrushchev's vision had a certain grandeur, and a certain plausibility, in the late fifties, when the first sputniks, and the early results of a more rational investment policy, fostered exaggerated notions of Soviet economic potential. In the event, the Soviet Union maintained the deterrent balance between itself and the United States (though in the middle sixties it began to fall behind in the development of space technology). But, after initial

successes, the results of Khrushchev's costly agricultural programmes were disappointing. A chronically inflexible and clumsy
planning system, and the disruptive effects of Khrushchev's continual reorganizations, retarded industrial growth. In the sixties
the Soviet economic achievement began to look less impressive
than that of the surgent capitalist countries, West Germany and
Japan. Khrushchev's ebullient, naive sincerity and demagogic flair
won him many admirers abroad, but brought no access of strength
to communist parties. Newly independent countries in Asia and
Africa readily accepted Soviet friendship and economic aid. The
international behaviour, and domestic policies, of some of them
was commended by the Soviet Union in novel formulae: they had
'taken the path of non-capitalist development', or even the
'socialist road'. But in most of these countries organized communism made no progress, and in some it was outlawed. And the
solid anti-imperialist front which Khrushchev had envisaged
proved to be a mirage.

Khrushchev's doctrinal innovations had helped him to
manoeuvre more freely in his foreign policy. His overriding object
was to alter the balance of world power in favour of the Soviet
Union by means short of war. Above all, he sought to free the
Soviet Union from the ring of advanced American bases. The
settlement of the German problem, détente in Europe, disarma-
ment proposals were all means to this end. Diplomatic initiatives
and peace propaganda with a wide public appeal were useful
methods of bringing pressure to bear on the United States, and
perhaps to loosen its alliances. But Khrushchev attached supreme
importance to continuous dialogue with the United States itself:
without American concessions he would make little headway.
Moreover, the dialogue enabled him to defuse the dangerously
tense situations which his initiatives might create. For 'means short
of war', in Khrushchev's interpretation, excluded neither sabre-
rattling nor even brinkmanship. Indeed, periodic reminders of
Soviet power, and of the perpetual risk of a nuclear clash, were
part of his technique: most riskily applied in 1962, when a Soviet
attempt to instal rocket bases in Cuba led to a hair-raising con-
frontation with the United States.

Khrushchev's legitimation of the parliamentary road to
socialism, and his reiterated denials of any ambition to 'export
revolution', were of course a (belated) recognition of political
realities in developed capitalist countries. They also, however,

gave the Soviet Union greater freedom of action in relations with bourgeois governments. Thus, while the French communists had full permission to concentrate on the task of winning elections, the Soviet Union developed ever warmer relations with General de Gaulle (and his successors). In France, this duality in Soviet policy had no effect on the public stance of a remarkably conservative communist leadership, nor on the behaviour of their supporters many of whom, as opinion surveys invariably demonstrate, cast their votes against the political establishment and the *patronat*, without wanting a communist dictatorship or necessarily accepting the Soviet version of international relations. Elsewhere, and notably in Italy, communists gratefully accepted their new and more promising role, felt less and less committed to Soviet ideological leadership, and were often openly critical of Soviet behaviour.

The effect of Khrushchev's unorthodoxy was a further weakening of Soviet authority in the world Communist movement. His attempts, at international communist conferences in 1957 and 1960, to find a formula which would reconcile limited local autonomy with effective Soviet leadership, failed miserably. The more important foreign parties signed nebulous declarations, and went their own ways. In the meantime, Khrushchev had brought upon himself a quarrel with the second largest and most powerful Communist Party.

In 1956–7 the Chinese, though irritated by the Twentieth Congress, supported Khrushchev's measures to hold the socialist camp together. They did so because they hoped to share leadership of a united camp, because they needed Soviet help to attain the main objects of their foreign policy (and especially to incorporate Taiwan) and because Soviet economic aid was essential to Chinese industrial development. In all these matters the Soviet Union fell short of Chinese expectations. It showed no disposition to concert foreign policy with China, or to accord China a leading role even in the Far East. It gave conspicuously grudging support during the off-shore islands crisis of 1958. It refused to help China in the development of atomic weapons. Soviet technical and industrial aid was, in Chinese eyes, inadequate and costly. Vociferous Soviet support of China's cause in the United Nations could not compensate for these offences. Equally ineffectual was Khrushchev's suggestion at the Twenty First Congress of the CPSU in 1958, that while the Soviet Union must for the present concentrate on developing itself, it would at some point 'close the gap' between the socialist countries so that they would all 'enter communism' more or less together.

The Chinese at first directed their fire against revisionist Yugoslavia, while the first onslaught on the Soviet Union came from incorrigibly Stalinist Albania, which sought protection against Yugoslav and Soviet pressures in an understanding with China. By 1962 relations between the major communist powers were so bad that the Russians openly supported India against Chinese encroachment on its borderlands. In the course of the sixties a propaganda war developed more vicious by far than that which each country simultaneously waged with the United States. The Soviet Union variously denounced Mao and his group as petty-bourgeois anarchists, Trotskyists and heirs of Genghis Khan and Hitler. The Chinese depicted the Soviet Union as a corrupt and privilege-ridden society, ruled by a bureaucratic caste which had abandoned the cause of revolution and the ideals of socialism, and which aimed at world hegemony in partnership with the United States. Hostilities were not always merely verbal. The Chinese, though they had recovered the ports and the railway retained by the Soviet Union under the 1950 Treaty, laid claim to extensive territories ceded under 'unequal treaties' to Tsarist Russia, and frontier clashes occurred on the Ussuri River.

The Chinese entered into direct competition with the Soviet Union both for leadership of the communist movement and for influence in the developing countries. They won qualified and fluctuating support in Korea, Japan and North Vietnam, and firmer support from the Indonesian Communist Party – the largest of all non-ruling parties until its destruction after the military coup of 1965. Pro-Chinese factions split from the old parties in many countries. In the third world the Chinese obtained a firm footing only in Africa. Their progress was checked by limited resources, and also by the domestic and international effects of the 'cultural revolution' in China itself. Their major success was to aggravate the Soviet Union's difficulties in asserting its leadership of the world movement. After the fall of Khrushchev in October 1964 his successors made a vain effort to patch up the quarrel. Thereafter, they worked doggedly, and also in vain, to convene a world Communist conclave which would excommunicate the Chinese leaders. Some of the major parties attended the 1969 Moscow conference only on the understanding that no act of excommunication would be introduced. The Italians, and some other Western parties, though they have not been spared Chinese abuse as revisionists and opportunists, and though they show a tactful preference for the Soviet case, have none the less found in the split occasions for a further display of independence. Even in Eastern Europe the quarrel has not only stiffened Albanian resistance to the Soviet Union but has emboldened Roumania to follow a maverick course.

In their polemics with the Soviet Union the Chinese have evolved an idiosyncratic ideology which, whatever its intrinsic merits, at least succeeds in casting doubt on the Marxist–Leninist orthodoxy of the Soviet Union. They claim a purer devotion to the struggle against imperialism. As they profess to see it, the Soviet Union is now merely another imperialistic great power. The struggle is now one between 'the world village' and 'the world city' – the underdeveloped and the developed countries. They refuse to identify socialism with a high level of economic development: the decisive criteria are to be sought in the class structure of society, in relations between the masses and the political leaders. The Soviet Union is travelling in the opposite direction from socialism: a hierarchy of privileges and rewards deepens and perpetuates the contradictions between town and country, between intellectual and physical labour, rulers and ruled. They, the Chinese, run no risk of bourgeois degeneration. For them, moral incentives are more important than material rewards, workers and intellectuals are interchangeable, individualism is not allowed to corrupt the collectivist spirit.

The Chinese blend of Leninist fundamentalism and pre-Leninist Utopianism is in part a matter of temporary convenience. Some foreign observers of China have lost sight of the cautionary example of the Webbs who saw the Soviet Union in the thirties as a 'new civilization'. There is much for them to ponder in the recent evolution of Chinese foreign policy. For the best of reasons – fear of the Soviet Union – the Chinese government is skilfully playing the power game in its foreign policy: seeking to offset the Soviet threat by rapprochement with the United States, adjusting its relations with other countries, and foreign political parties, not according to revolutionary principle, but according to their relations with the Soviet Union. Nor can the pattern of social relationships in China, even if it is accurately depicted in Chinese and Sino–Webbist accounts, remain unaffected as the economy grows stronger and more complex.

177